Advances in Organization Development

Volume 2

edited by

Fred Massarik

ABLEX PUBLISHING CORPORATION
NORWOOD, NEW JERSEY

Printed in the United States of America.

Library of Congress Cataloging-in-Publication Data

Advances in organization development / edited by Fred Massarik.
    p. cm.
    Includes bibliographical references.
    ISBN 0–89391–809–1 (v. 2)
    1. Organizational change.   I. Massarik, Fred.
  HD58.8.A38 1989
  658.4′06—dc20
                                         89–17852
                                          CIP

Ablex Publishing Corporation
355 Chestnut St.
Norwood, NJ 07648

Contents

Preface

Organization Development continues to develop. This unfolding proceeds significantly in practice—together with some widening impact of theoretic reflection, and in a climate of frequent soul-searching and self-examination. See, for instance, Susan Albers Mohrman's "Some Thoughts on Organization Development in Transition" (Academy of Management ODC NEWSLETTER, Summer 1992), and Jack Cantwell's "Organization Development: What It May Have Meant" (OD PRACTITIONER vol. 24, no. 1, March 1992).

Excerpting Mohrman's paper:

> Are we selling our soul in search of rigor? Are we relevant? Are we rigorous enough? Are we sticking to the principles that were the foundation of our field? Is this a field? Do we still have a common foundation?

And Cantwell, by way of gentle futuristic satire:

> We can say with at least some degree of accuracy that (OD) died out sometime in either the late twentieth or early twenty-first centuries.

Our view is neither Demise nor Apocalypse Now, but Ferment—efforts to rethink, to realign, to redefine in a world of change beyond bounds and borders—together with everyday efforts, hands-on, in helping people and complex systems to make better things happen humanly and humanely—all the way from the individual to the daunting sweeps of organizations within a turbulent society.

The simplicity of the past—if indeed it every prevailed at all—surely is history. But steering between the Scylla of nostalgia ("process is the *only* thing") to the Charybdis of megalomania ("OD will change *The World*"), there evolves the continuing and responsible effort of a growing profession to find its way and to strengthen its impact—consciously, capably, and (we shall hope) caringly.

It is in this context that this second volume of *Advances in Organization Development* makes its appearance. It continues in its orientation, initially noted in Vol. 1, to provide new perspectives and viewpoints, in concept and theory as well as in application and practice. In its themes, the following may be discerned:

- The profession in broad perspective, including internal conflict and ethics (Massarik, "Paradox and Process . . .", Gellermann, "Issues on the Frontier . . .")
- Innovative conceptual and practice approaches (Goldstein, "Beyond Lewin's Force Field . . ."; Pauchant, "In Search of Existence . . ."; Vogt, "Networks . . ."; Culbert & McDonough, "Trusting Relationships . . . Truth Telling)
- Consideration of "Culture" as an issue in OD (Lövey, "Some Issues . . . Reflections from Hungary")
- Personal and professional viewpoints on OD styles (Luft, "The Other Impossible Profession"; Kingsbury, "How to Use Laboratory Learning") and
- Relationships between OD and other fields (Colarelli, "Organization Development and Personnel Psychology . . .")

May the contents of this volume in some sense prove to be true to its name, advancing the field's directions, and adding to its evident vitality. Far from moribund, sometimes surprisingly (even—some may say—disconcertingly) mainstream, and in persistent search for new approaches, Organization Development has much work ahead in the mid-1990s and beyond.

If you want to contribute to this task by submitting a manuscript for consideration and possible publication in *Advances in Organization Development*, Vol. 3 or Vol. 4, please contact the editor of this volume at an early convenience. Our shared dialogue *can* make a difference as we seek to link thought and concept to action and to the enhancement of human well-being.

Fred Massarik
Anderson Graduate School
  of Management
UCLA
Los Angeles, CA

1

Paradox and Process: Facing Internal Methods Conflicts in Organization Development

Fred Massarik
Anderson Graduate School of Management
UCLA

"You've got to be right—but you've got to be fast too. . . ."
   (Paraphrased from a famous quiz show.)

"To be as beautiful as the birds, we need time . . . just time."
   (From an old German proverb.)

Even the process of change is changing. We have spoken of chaos. We have reflected on uncertainty and on the notion that all kinds of ambiguity are here to stay. All this upheaval sets the stage for various paradoxical conditions in organization development, and, at the same time, for unprecedented opportunity.

It is evident to all—in and outside the field of OD—that the 1990s have begun as a decade of monumental transformation. Gorbachev's *Perestroika*, having survived the failed August 1991 coup, in part reads like an OD text. Whatever happens in Europe, 1993 and beyond, the realignments of social and economic power on the Continent, together with the free-market capitalization of former Eastbloc nations and complex shifts in corporate and national governance most everywhere, establish a remarkable macrocontext for organization development. Events of this kind constitute pervasive background and effect rapid and profound change as well at conceptual mid-range and micro levels, in corporate and other organization systems and in individual dynamics within them.

With these trepidations and oscillations co-acting at all levels, the very quality of the change process, both spontaneous and planned, shifts. It goes beyond the accustomed quasi-equilibria, and it calls for more rapid, yet insightful and effective response by OD practitioners and change agents than may have been normally expected in earlier times. And with this new "change climate" moving ahead, accented perhaps by intermittent periods of consolidation, this cannot be an occasion for "business as usual" in a profession that, at its core, is committed to change itself. There are, however, contradictions present that may impede broad-scale responsiveness in the new rapid-change environment as indicated. Sorting out these contradictions may be worth a try as we look to the next stage in the development of Organization Development.

EXAMINING SOME CONTRADICTIONS WITHIN ORGANIZATION DEVELOPMENT

Many competent OD practitioners will agree that OD is committed to process. Surely the very concept of process consultation speaks to this: Consultation addressing among members of a team or within a larger client system obviously involves the OD practitioner in a time-extensive process in his or her varied role. And indeed this extension over time—sometimes a good deal of time—cannot be cut short without impeding the process itself; in other words, "you can't push the river." Anyone involved in small-group training (T-groups, some kinds of team building, leadership development, interpersonal communication) knows tacitly that some events, including necessary frustrations, need to precede mature "work" and successful closure. Accordingly, time remains a powerful variable, one that often is seen as intractable.

On the other hand, what we have said about the prevalence of rapid change suggests a need for relatively accelerated intervention types. Perhaps now OD needs to work more quickly than ever, and it needs to generate a sense of forward movement and evident success, contravening the traditional linear approach, such as prework, diagnosis, intervention design, intervention, and evaluation—each neatly following the other.

There are, of course, OD "products" that do not fit totally within either the process or quick-response models, models which in themselves are, at least on the surface, in conflict with one another. Those approaches that simply "do a workshop" on an organization-relevant topic without more than nominal preanalysis or diagnosis, and those that simply conclude without follow-up, avoid (evade) the dilemma. Likewise, "canned," off-the-shelf intervention packages, calling for direct administration with little preparatory activity or involvement after the package has been delivered, fall in this category.

From both a theoretical and practical viewpoint one needs to ask "what's best now?" As we consider the several alternative intervention models noted, ranging from extensive process and its time commitments to quick and rapid response, and the inherent trade-offs, it is obvious that no simple answer suffices; the key remains case-by-case analysis of the client system's needs. Still, what we know about complex systems suggests that *the process component remains of intrinsically central importance, and that short-term interventions, however structured and delivered, need to be lodged within the process context noted.* Thus, with rapid change upon the land and time pressures heightened, OD practice confronts the requirement to reconcile the integrity of process with demands for quick and efficacious response.

EFFORTS TO RECONCILE

Long-term process has many facets in systems that are subject to change in themselves. Within a small group it may be circumscribed by that group's lifetime, whether naturally or artificially defined. In a larger social system, such as an organization, it may continue for the life of that organization, over years, decades and beyond, with a changing membership at various levels of the hierarchy, including the top. And within the larger organization system there are nested subsystems (e.g., subsidiaries, divisions, plants, work groups, and their related informal interpersonal constellations) that each have their own lifetimes. Accordingly, there is not a "single long-term process" that speaks to events across the entire spectrum; rather, such process needs to be viewed in context of a set of time-extensive systems having life spans of varying durability. In times of rapid changes as currently exist, this durability and continuity is subject to greater variation than had been the case previously.

As these natural systems changes vary and fluctuate (for example, in aftermath of mergers, downsizing, department reorganizations, spin-offs, etc.) the OD practitioner must also remain nimble, and is challenged to keep up with these quickly shifting events. Rapid diagnosis and potential redefinition of task becomes, for the *process-oriented* OD practitioner, a manifest requirement. In some ways those practitioners who market a specific "product," simply delivering it without much concern for process background, may well have an easier time of it—the "workshop" runs its day and a half, the participants approve/disapprove, learn or fail to learn, and the event is completed. If benefits have accrued, these are brought back to the world at home, such as the system(s) within which the

FIGURE 1.1.

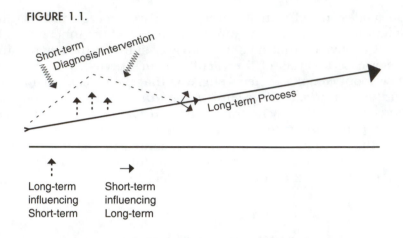

participant works or lives, in context of subsystems that themselves have undergone natural change in the meantime.

It becomes useful to propose a conceptual framework that involves the simultaneous progression of both underlying time-extension *process* within the organization system or subsystem *and short-term* diagnosis and intervention.

The nature of this framework is shown in Figure 1.1.

As the long-term process follows its course, the short-term events are lodged within it and interact with it, in a context of mutual interinfluence. The short-term interventions are not simply superimposed but directly and indirectly feed into the nature of long-term process.

If one considers the nature of the interaction between long-term process and short-term diagnosis and intervention, it becomes clear that as even long-term process becomes less stable, that is, under present conditions of rapid change, the amount of instability increases in still greater measure, at a more than simply additive rate. The nature of this process calls for empirical verification. The framework, however, might be viewed as follows in Figure 1.2.

The interactions are likely to be more complex, and further challenge the OD practitioner as she or he wishes to assure that the combination of long-term development *and* short-term diagnosis and intervention becomes appropriate for the needs of a system or subsystem. If one imagines as a metaphor an old car with wheels out of alignment speeding along a bumpy road, one may look for a driver who has an especially solid grasp of the wheel, and who can make quick and responsive adjustments to the bumps and bounces along the roadway.

FIGURE 1.2.

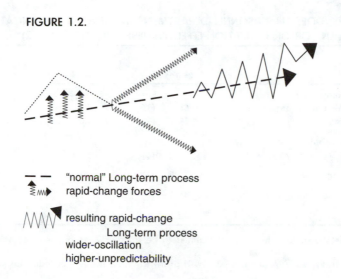

- - - "normal" Long-term process
rapid-change forces

resulting rapid-change
    Long-term process
wider-oscillation
higher-unpredictability

Given the above considerations the issue does not become one of whether one should attend *either* to long-term process *or* to short-term interventions, leaving out one or the other. Minimally, the OD practitioner with a valid long-term view of organization and professional task needs to diagnose expediently what is going on in the larger system as it moves along, often more quickly than anticipated, upon the hazard-strewn roads of the present socioeconomic and organizational environment.

In this frame, two questions arise:

1. What are the chances of developing more effective opportunities for the Development of Organization Development in these changing environments?, and
2. Is it possible to find more effective ways for responsive short-term, "high-intensity" diagnosis, to keep up with more rapid changes in systems process?

OD'S POSITION IN CORPORATE SETTINGS

For starters, let us attempt some assessment of OD's present position in a set of corporate settings, as an index to OD's future viability within such systems. By way of illustration—and with no claim for universal generalizability—we take a look at major companies in the *computer and high technology, environment and energy technology,* and *transportation* sectors. For these, all involving rapid technologic and organizational change, we may ask: Is an OD function, broadly defined, to be found in these settings? Is it pervasive? Rare?

TABLE 1.1.   DOES HR/PERSONNEL DEPARTMENT INCLUDE AN ORGANIZATION DEVELOPMENT OR ORGANIZATION EFFECTIVENESS FUNCTION? (Q.12)*

		% Yes	(n)	% No	(n)	% Total
	Computer & High Tech**					
A_1	Medium & large	68.2	(15)	31.8	(7)	100.0
A_2	small	39.2	(20)	60.8	(31)	100.0
	Environment and Energy					
B	Technology	46.2	(6)	53.8	(7)	100.0
C	Transportation	38.5	(5)	61.5	(8)	100.0
D,E,F	Various Industries	42.1	(8)	57.9	(11)	100.0
TOTAL		45.8	(54)	54.2	(64)	100.0

(Totals shown for reference, not claimed to be rigorously responsive of other industry groups.)

* This study was supported in part by a grant from the Institute of Industrial Relations, UCLA.

** A_1 approx. 12,000 to 120,000 employees

A_2 under 12,000 employees

And what does the term "Organization Development" or "Organization Effectiveness" connote in this context?

We focus on the human resources/personnel departmental operations in these settings, based on a 1990–91 telephone survey conducted at the Anderson Graduate School of Management, UCLA, reaching 118 top ranking Human Resource/Personnel executives. Basic findings are shown in Table 1.1.

For industry types examined, it appears that somewhat less than half, yet quite a considerable percentage (45.8%), indicate that an Organization Development or Organization Effectiveness function exists in the HR/Personnel department operations noted.

The percentage of affirmative responses was particularly high for medium and large computer and high-tech companies—68.2%— and relatively smaller for small companies in this sector as well as for those in transportation. One may conjecture that company size makes a difference, and not unreasonably, with larger HR departments and organization systems having more capability for sustaining such functions, based on economies of scale and on probable demand for their services. However, we find some industry specificity: Transportation, though it involves large company size, shows relatively lower proportions of OD/OE presence (38.5%).

While, of course, one cannot assume identical results across industry types or industrial sectors, these findings suggest that there is quite a significant presence of OD/OE in organization systems which themselves are undergoing major natural change.

While the study as a whole focused on the HR/Personnel profession itself, the relatively widespread appearance of OD/OE within Human Resources operations suggests the presence of a promising window of opportunity. In part, this window relates to the very ambiguity with which OD/OE is perceived by the HR/Personnel executives studied. Some quotations from these interviews are of interest:

- (OD) . . . that's me! I'm concerned (as part of my HR job) with performance and motivation . . . and with what all this means for the firm's long-term objectives.
  (service industry company, 5,000 employees)

- (This company) traditionally has been committed to OD. . . . We play a role in Quality Improvement Programs. . . . We won a Malcolm Baldridge award in 1989. . . . Much of what we do is focused on organization effectiveness and quality.
  (Well-established computer and office technology company, 110,000 employees)

- Yes, there is OD at the corporate HR level . . . mainly training and development and executive development.
  (computer company, formed as result of a merger, 90,000 employees)

- OD exists here. . . . It does a variety of things having to do with people and their effectiveness. . . . It's internally decentralized and also works with (a nearby college); it's a critical part of HR here and reports to the VP/HR.
  (diversified computer and office equipment company, 33,000 employees)

- We have OD. . . . It's hard to say just how influential it is . . . but it does (influence) cultural change at the mid-level. . . . We use project teams to improve management skills. . . . We help to provide feedback purposes of product development.
  (computer chip company, 15,000 employees)

- (OD) here is mainly training and development for high-potential people and hiring for our international business.
  (small computer "clone" company, 2,000 employees)

- It's training and development . . . to improve the skill level of workers . . . workshops, etc.
  (small computer company, 2,200 employees)

It becomes clear that OD in practice means many things to many people and companies from one-person operations to complex system-wide efforts. One theme that recurs focuses on "training and development" either as synonymous with OD or as the OD contact point. From the study as a whole the following themes are identified. OD is or involves:

- Training and development/executive development
- Efforts to improve performance and motivation
- Quality improvement
- Cultural change
- Team development
- Overall concern for people

This is not a neat definitive pattern of themes. It includes very broad statements having to do with something like "good things for people" to fairly specific approaches and their implementation, such as quality improvement and team development. What is lacking is any semblance to conventional textbook definitions such as "planned change by behavioral science methods" and the like, or at least HR/Personnel executives do not spontaneously think in these terms. If there is a more common theme it relates to the "training and development function."

One might choose to lament this ambiguity. It does, however, generate a set of propositions as follows:

- a fair amount of activity that might be described as OD/OE (at least in terms of the interview formulation) *is* going on;
- what *is* going on is quite variable and "sails under many flags"; perhaps the most visible of these is "training and development" as umbrella or, in some instances, as label;
- an "interest in people," in some form, serves as backdrop and rationale, but many activities are subsumed and OD/OE itself rarely appears as the salient core of what is going on;
- thus, the pattern of themes emerges that is ambiguous and varied, but there is activity and interest; we conclude that all this provides a climate of openness to new means of OD/OE-type diagnosis and intervention.

Circumstances as cited may account for the proliferation of OD-type "packages" and readily deliverable interventions. In perspective, in the face of rapid external and internal change, it seems that

the companies covered are, in high if not always majority propor-
tion, committed to the people area, with no rigid boundaries defined. This suggests that opportunities for further growth of OD-
type interventions, whatever their definitions, continue to prevail—
perhaps more than ever.

BUT WHAT KIND OF OD?

Let us return to the notion of the paradox previously sketched: the
apparent contradiction between commitment to time-extensive process and the need for rapidly responsive, quickly available diagnosis
and intervention. We have suggested in a previous section that
"process" constitutes a long-term strand of interpersonal events,
itself perhaps being more irregular and speeded up these days than
before. At the same time, short-term diagnosis and intervention
interacts with long-term process, in ways which are not always clear
and call out for systematic research.

The interactions between short-term interventions and long-term
process are necessarily iterative and conceptually interlocked; they
are not two separate parallel tracks that pass one another in the
night, and yet, in the rapid-change world it is particularly important
to pay attention to short-term diagnosis (itself a kind of intervention) as basis for proximate intervention strategies.

In the present state, short-term OD interventions (fairly brief
workshops, exercises, presentations and didactic inputs to management programs, case discussions, etc.) abound. Fewer cases exist
relating to short-term diagnosis. Such diagnostic efforts are defined
here as follows: Short-term diagnosis involves systematic means for
determining, within a time frame of one month or less, the nature of
the underlying problem (organization, systems, interpersonal, etc.),
as possible contrast to the presenting problem (as initially stated, by
client and/or OD practitioner), by utilization of patterns of key data
points, as basis for prompt follow-up intervention—with positive
results anticipated within a projected (and often short-term) time
horizon, that is, within a time frame ranging from weeks to three to
four months.

Such short-term diagnosis does not permit the luxury (or expense) of more traditional diagnostic means such as often-
cumbersome large-scale attitude surveys or extensive interview programs, which themselves may require months. Yet, is short-term
diagnosis to be regarded as involving haphazard short cuts, simply
to save time? Here the word "systematic" must be emphasized.

Accordingly, the following framework for short-term diagnosis and its antecedents is proposed:

1. It is recognized that the OD practitioner comes to the task with a conceptual framework, based on past experience and theoretic structuring of what's ahead. These conceptual maps need to be explicit, and need to be valued as establishing parameters for subsequent diagnosis. This step may be translated into the development of rough-idea scenarios, describing (or speculating on) various things that might have happened in the past and that might occur in the future. These scenarios need not be "right" (knowing, of course, that there is no single "right" definition in most instances, but they are heavily subject to differential perception); however, such scenarios provide some groundwork for what is to follow, even though they are substantially less-than-perfect, or indeed faulty.

2. "Doing homework" is necessary on paper or other preexisting (including database) materials available in the organization system. This step, itself based on initial client contact, drawing on published and generally available materials, calls for selectivity. . . . It does not propose that huge reams of materials need to be analyzed in most instances, whereas critical items, including the verbal and nonverbal messages of annual reports, house organs, available memoranda, etc., provide "going-in clues."

3. With "homework" and scenarios in hand, the OD practitioner develops a new set of *key data points*. These may vary widely in nature and form; they may include *individuals* to be interviewed, *observations* to be made in situ, *participation* in upcoming meetings and/or *perceptions of meeting processes* by key individuals, and the like.

These key data points are not static in their patterning. While data points are delineated roughly as quickly as possible at the beginning of the diagnosis, projected key data points may be dropped or new ones added as data collection proceeds, considering the changing context. This method resembles aspects of humanistic research and the concept of "saturation," suggesting that after certain convergences in data arise these can be chronicled and additional data collection can be reduced or terminated. *Successive corroboration* becomes useful.

Further, it is not assumed that only a single OD practitioner functions in this mode. Several may be active simultaneously, with assignment to a variety of key data points and purposefully planned "on-line" cross-checking among the set of evolving observations, within short time frames specified.

4. As key data points have been covered by one or more of the OD

practitioners, namely, observers, and as initial *trial diagnosis* is in hand, this trial diagnosis provides a basis for direct input to a broadened *team* including key persons within the organization system (some of whom may indeed have been involved as interviewees in the key data point set) and the OD practitioner(s). At this stage while the events involved in the short-term diagnosis themselves constitute an intervention type, as is widely recognized, there now follows quick roll-over into other interventions. Each of these is in turn diagnostic in some way, as soon as some awareness of the intervention's process and outcome is available.

5. As these short term diagnostic/intervention linkages go forward, the broader system itself is changing, as it were, by "natural causes" which interact with those relating to the OD/OE program in action. It is evident that actual organizational outcomes are a multicausal product of which the OD diagnostic/intervention process is only one element. Whether confined to a small subsystem within a large organization or whether aspiring "total systems" change or "culture change", all these events, *in seriatim* and in-flow, must be understood in light of broader enveloping changes at all levels—economic, technological, social, environmental, and the like. If we are to evaluate the impact of a given OD program we must necessarily be enmeshed in this complex interplay between whatever is provided by the OD practitioner(s) and by the enveloping macro-systems, simultaneously and interactively.

Short-term diagnosis calls for careful conceptual prework and for highly active implementation based on design which by its nature is iterative and subject to successive changes. Thereafter, its emerging template moves quickly into subsequent intervention modes, responsive to the projected rapid changes evident within and about the system.

REVISITING PROCESS AND TRUST

It is this chapter's contention that long-term process needs to be recognized in the face of need for short-term diagnosis and intervention. Such long-term process is based on the much emphasized variables of trust and relationship, between key persons in the organization system and the OD practitioner(s). While recently the subject of some controversy, it is this chapter's position that top management support, ranging from tacit to fully involved, remains a necessary condition for effective OD implementation and outcome, as long as systems are constructed in hierarchical form. Whatever the issue here, long-term process is lined closely to long-term trust and to associated long-term relationships among all concerned.

With rapid change, of course, relationships may be suddenly terminated as people leave or move to other jobs, as companies are liquidated, and as subsidiaries merge or are divested. It is all the more important that what still may provide continuity is nurtured and valued, as an integrative force in the maelstrom. Short-term diagnosis and intervention, let's recall, interacts within this more time-extensive network of process, involving trust and relationship among those concerned with the organization's long-term welfare.

Thus the paradox is resolved: Short-term and long-term are part of the same fabric, and as change proceeds in quick and often unpredictable contour, the need for fundamental theoretic understanding and practical conduct of trust and relationship give basic impetus for positive change in a world that won't quit changing.

Further, as a practical matter, though we have reemphasized the well-seasoned assertion that top management support (at least of some kind) is essential, we need to revisit the role of the Human Resources/Personnel department. As our findings have shown, at least in the industries reviewed here, there is much going on that ambiguously leaves the road open to Organization Development opportunities, whether under the "training and development" heading or by various euphemisms (e.g., "education and growth," "organization effectiveness," etc.). The Human Resource/Personnel department can become the locus par excellence for trust and relationship development as the basis for long-term process required by successful OD development in changing systems. While recessions and economic fluctuations undoubtedly take their toll, over the longer time span the increased informed involvement of top Human Resources/Personnel executives, both in understanding of OD's approach and of its modes of diagnosis and intervention, is of major importance. In turn, the OD practitioner, whether internal or external, needs to understand the turbulent realities and strategic considerations of entire patterns of systems, not only in the Human Resources area, but as well within the broader context of management in national, cultural and worldwide realignments that, in waves of change, characterize the present era.

REFERENCES

Bakan, D. (1967). *On method*. San Francisco: Jossey-Bass.
Bush, K. (Ed.). (1990). *From the command economy to the market*. London: Dartmouth Publishing.

Carroll, H.D. (1990, Spring). Perestroika in the American Corporation. *Organizational Dynamics*, pp. 4–21.

Glaser, B.G, & Strauss, A.L. (1967). *The discovery of grounded theory.* Chicago: Aldine Publishing.

Gorbachev, M. (1987). *Perestroika*. New York: Harper & Row.

London, M. (1988). *Change agents.* San Francisco: Jossey-Bass.

RFE/RL Research Institute. (1991). *Report on Eastern Europe.* New York: RFE/RL.

Roeber, R.J.C. (1973). *The organization in a changing environment.* Reading, MA: Addison-Wesley.

Schein, E.H. (1969). *Process consultation—Its role in organization development.* Reading, MA: Addison-Wesley.

2

Organization Development and Personnel Psychology: Issues and Integration

Stephen M. Colarelli
Central Michigan University

It is curious and unfortunate that organization development (OD) and personnel psychology (PP) have not become closely allied fields. It is curious because PP technologies—personnel selection, job analysis, training, and performance appraisal—are behavioral science technologies, and most definitions of OD include the planned application of behavioral science technologies in personal and organizational contexts. It is also curious because the implementation of any PP technology involves issues central to OD—resistance to change, interpersonal competence, group dynamics, and communication.

It is unfortunate that there is so little interconnection between OD and PP because both fields help to create a skilled workforce, which is essential for American competitiveness in the twenty first century (Dertouzos, Lestor, & Solow, 1989). Managers and scholars alike recognize that PP technologies—especially personnel selection and training—are critical ingredients in making America competitive. Yet, most organizations in the United States are inept at using state-of-the-art PP technologies (Latham, 1988). Why is this so? One reason might be that PP does not deal with how to *implement* its technologies. Another reason might be that OD—in its approach and literature—largely has ignored PP. The time is ripe, therefore, to develop an organization development of personnel psychology.

This chapter has three purposes. I begin by discussing why there is so little integration between OD and PP; then I consider conceptually the possible integration of OD and PP. Finally, I suggest how we can encourage greater integration of the two fields.

WHY THERE IS LITTLE INTEGRATION
BETWEEN ORGANIZATION DEVELOPMENT
AND PERSONNEL PSYCHOLOGY

OD and PP have been associated with different types of behavioral science technologies. For example, we associate OD with team building, process consultation, T-groups, and survey feedback. On the other hand, we associate PP with employment tests, skill training, and performance appraisal rating scales. I would suggest, however, that it is not the technologies that distinguish OD from PP. Rather, what distinguishes OD from PP are differences in orientations about human nature, organizations, and clients; different historical backgrounds; and differences in the types of people who are attracted to the fields. I believe that these differences between OD and PP have remained implicit. By making them explicit, we make them accessible; and by making them accessible, we are in a better position to deal with these differences constructively.

Different Orientations

A standard definition of OD is a planned, organization-wide effort, managed from the top to increase organization effectiveness and organization health, through planned interventions in the organization's processes using behavioral science knowledge (Beckhard, 1969). PP is defined as the identification, measurement, and development of individual differences, within organizations, using behavioral science knowledge to increase individual satisfaction and performance. On the surface, PP could be included within OD. However, when one looks at the basic assumptions associated with the two fields, one begins to see why there has been so little integration. The two fields hold different assumptions about human nature, organizations, and approaches to clients.

Human nature. PP is concerned with attributes of individuals, and it views the individual in isolation of the group or system (Dunnette, 1966, 1976). OD, on the other hand, is concerned with the whole person, and it views the person as part of a group and system (French & Bell, 1984). Personnel psychology tends to deal with the cognitive aspects of people (Schmidt & Hunter, 1981), whereas OD attends to the emotional elements of people as well (e.g., Schein, 1969). While OD views people as changeable and capable of growth, PP views people as having relatively fixed characteristics (Dunnette, 1966).

The nature of organizations. PP views organizations as machines, whereas OD views organizations as open systems (Colarelli & Stumpf, 1990; Morgan, 1986). PP is oriented towards the *status quo*—towards making the current state of affairs more efficient (Argyris, 1976). OD, on the other hand, is oriented towards organizational *change* (Beer, 1980). With PP, the individual tends to be the fundamental unit of analysis; whereas with OD, the primary units of analysis typically are the dyad, group, and organization. PP tends to view organizations as the sum of their parts (Colarelli & Stumpf 1990). OD, on the other hand, takes a more synergistic approach, suggesting that the whole does not equal the sum of the parts, and that the whole is something different than the sum of its parts (Morgan, 1986). PP is concerned with content and measurement, whereas OD is concerned more with social psychological processes and with communication (Tichy, 1974). Finally, PP has not—until recently with the emergence of strategic human resource management—dealt with top management and strategic issues. It has concerned itself with personnel department and middle management issues. OD, on the other hand, deals more with top management and top management concerns.

Relationships with clients. Personnel psychologists view their role primarily as technical experts who provide advice to managers or personnel managers (London & Moses, 1990). Another role of personnel psychologists is that of a "pair of hands." In this role, the personnel psychologist performs the technical jobs that the manager or client requests, such as implementing an employee testing or appraisal system. The OD consultant, on the other hand, takes a facilitator role, and attempts to work collaboratively with the client (Burke, 1982). The personnel psychologist emphasizes his or her specialized knowledge and technical skills. The OD consultant does as well, but also emphasizes interpersonal skills, consulting skills, and—more recently—political skills (Burke, 1982; Greiner & Schein, 1988).

Other differences between personnel psychologists and OD consultants relate to their approachs to legal issues, their views of applied science, and their orientations toward time. PP, particularly in the area of personnel selection, is concerned with the law (Arvey, 1979; Ledvinka & Scarpello, 1991). Some of PP's focus on employment law is unavoidable. The passage of the Civil Rights Act of 1964, the establishment of the Equal Employment Opportunity Commission, and the development of the *Uniform Guidelines on Employee Selection*, have forced employment law into PP. While this means that personnel psychologists need to stay current of legal issues, the field has gone overboard and embraced litigiousness. Unfortunately, a legal frame of reference erects barriers; and the legal orientation of PP can make it difficult for personnel psychologists and managers to collaborate in a problem-solving manner. In fact, some observers suggest that the excessive legalism in the United States seriously hampers organizational effectiveness:

> Compared with the Japanese, Americans have elevated legal due process into a virtual fetish. Today, few large projects can be undertaken in the United States without endless hearings and appeals. . . . Many Japanese observers regard the American adversarial system as inefficient, obnoxious, and even irrational. They wonder how business ever gets done in America, and they note with amusement that it sometimes doesn't get done at all. (McCraw, 1986, p. 27)

On the other hand, personnel psychologists can use employment law to pressure organizations to change (cf. Tichy, 1974). Many of the fair employment practices that organizations outwardly embrace would have been slower in coming were it not for legal pressure (cf. Levitt, 1968).

OD consultants usually have little legal orientation. Collaboration and mutual problem solving are the essence of OD consulting. It is almost unheard of for OD consultants to use outside pressure to effect change. In this respect, OD's emphasis on collaboration resembles the Japanese approach to business. However, this can also limit the capacity of OD practitioners to effect societal change (Tichy, 1974).

Personnel psychologists subscribe to the scientist/practitioner model of consulting (Society for Industrial and Organizational Psychology, Inc., 1985). The central characteristic of this model is a research orientation to practice: Consultants should use only behavioral science technologies that have hard data to back up their validity, and they should rigorously evaluate their interventions. OD consultants appear to follow more of a straight consulting model (cf. Beer & Walton, 1987). The OD consultant bases interventions on behavioral science research *and* theory (Beer & Walton, 1987). The OD consultant is more likely to use an intervention that may be lacking empirical support, but grounded in theory.

OD practitioners are somewhat skeptical of traditional methods for evaluating behavioral science technologies (Beer & Walton, 1987). They view the practice of OD as an art as well as a science. The OD consultant seems to see his or her role, in part, as one of shaping a reality within given organizational constraints (Eden,

1986), whereas the personnel psychologist is interested in peeling away layers of "fluff" to get to the "truth."

The two fields also differ in their time perspective. OD takes a long-term perspective in working with the client and implementing an intervention (Beer & Walton, 1987). PP has a shorter time perspective. The personnel psychologist's goal is to install an intervention that solves a problem. PP's long-term perspective is with the research underlying its technologies.

Different Historical Backgrounds

PP and OD began at different times in history, in response to different events, with different casts of characters, and in different intellectual and cultural milieus. Modern PP began at the turn of the century. American industry was rapidly expanding, and needed to select and train masses of immigrants for semiskilled jobs. The names most personnel psychologists often associate with the early development of their field are Hugo Munsterberg (Moskowitz, 1977) and Frederick Taylor.

Hugo Munsterberg. Munsterberg—a German emigré recruited to Harvard by William James in 1892—was interested in applying the principles of psychology to industry to improve efficiency and worker well-being. Some of Munsterberg's ideas are still prominent in PP today: breaking down jobs into tasks and matching workers to jobs based on the fit between worker skills and job tasks; systematic training; focusing on means rather than ends; and leaving decisions about ends up to management. Unfortunately, Munsterberg's support of the German cause during World War I made him unpopular, and he died prematurely in 1916. As a result, he never fully developed a theoretical base for PP, nor did he develop a cadre of students to carry on his ideas.

Frederick Taylor. The other major figure in PP is Frederick Taylor. Taylor, an engineer by training, founded the school of thought called "scientific management" (Taylor 1911). Scientific management advocated the application of scientific principles to the study of work, and it claimed that these principles could improve efficiency, productivity, worker satisfaction, and harmony between workers and management. Given the large number of factory jobs at the time, Taylor was concerned with improving efficiency in unskilled and semiskilled jobs. Scientific management involved analyzing jobs, breaking them down to their smallest parts, conducting time and motion studies to improve the efficiency of manual work, using "one best way" to accomplish a job, matching the skill level of workers with the task requirements of the job, and rewarding work-ers for productive work.

Taylor focused on the individual; he had little regard or apprecia-tion for the work group. He believed that when "men work in gangs, their individual efficiency falls almost invariably down to, or below, the level of the worst man in the gang" (Taylor, 1911, pp. 71-72). Although he saw little use for workgroups, he did believe in friendly cooperation between management and workers. Taylor focused on *parts* of the job and *parts* of the person.

Scientific management reflected a mechanistic outlook that was characteristic of scientific thought from the "mechanical philoso-phers" of the seventeenth century—especially Descartes and Newton—to the early twentieth century (cf. Toulmin, 1990). Taylor has been a major and sustained influence on the field of PP, even up to the present day. His ideas have had a powerful influence on PP's view of jobs, its approach to job analysis and personnel selection, its mechanistic orientation, and PP's emphasis on the individual.

Kurt Lewin. Organization development's historical background is quite different. The beginnings of OD can be traced to the late 1940s and 1950s. One stem of OD began in 1946 with the laboratory training sessions in intergroup relations at New Britain, Connecti-cut, lead by Kurt Lewin. Lewin was a seminal figure in OD, as well as in organizational psychology and social psychology. Often referred to as "the practical theorist" (Marrow, 1969), Lewin emphasized the importance of applying social psychological theory to practical and social problems, through a process of action research. Although Lewin himself was a brilliant theorist, he was also interested in applying psychological theory to practical problems. As a Jewish emigré who fled Nazi Germany, Lewin had deep interests in groups and group identity, and in using psychology to help solve social and political problems (Marrow, 1969).

Lewin's field theory emphasized interpersonal, group, and inter-group relations. Many of the ideas in field theory were influenced by Gestalt psychology and quantum physics—emphasizing relations rather than elements, and probabilities rather than direct influence. In his classic paper on Aristotelian and Galilean modes of thought (Lewin, 1935), he argued that while the physical sciences had shifted from Aristotelian to Galilean thinking, psychology had still not made the shift. The problem with Aristotelian thinking was the notion that behavior is caused by properties residing *in* the individ-ual. Galileian thinking, on the other hand, emphasizes the dynamic forces causing behavior, and in particular the influence on the *relationships* between people or between the person and the situation. Although a pioneer in experimental social psychology (e.g., Lewin, Lippitt, & White, 1939), Lewin felt that a nonquantitative (nonquantitative in the way that Lewin used it) form of mathematics was necessary to represent spatial relationships in the psychological field. He used a branch of mathematics called topology.

The Hawthorne studies, Renis Likert, and others. Other significant influences—but by not means the only ones—on modern organization development were the Hawthorne studies (Roethlisberger & Dickson, 1939), and Renis Likert. The Hawthorne studies were an important precursor to OD because they documented the importance and influence of the informal organization on the individual, and the powerful role of the workgroup. Renis Likert and Floyd Mann of the University of Michigan's Institute for Social Research are credited with developing the widely used OD technique of survey feedback. Survey feedback is the most quantitative OD technique, but its historical influence on OD has less to do with quantitative methods than with its approach. Survey feedback was the first system-wide approach, gathering information from many levels of an organization and feeding it back to management. It is a classic example of action research: gathering data, preliminary diagnosis and feedback to management, stimulating change with information, collaborative problem solving between managers and consultants, organization-wide feedback, action-planning, and action. Another important contribution of the early survey work of Likert and Mann to OD was Mann's discovery that little change occurred when managers·failed to discuss the results of a survey with employees and plan collaboratively.

People Attracted to PP and OD and Their Clients

Given the differences in orientation and history between PP and OD, different types of people are likely to be attracted to the two fields. PP is quantitative and concerned with personnel systems; it involves minimal contact between the consultant and organization members. OD, on the other hand, is qualitative and concerned with interpersonal processes; it involves intensive personal contact between the consultant and organization members. Argyris (1976) has suggested that individuals who are more comfortable with numbers than people, and who are uneasy with close collaboration, tend to enter a field like PP. People who would be attracted to OD would be people-oriented, and indeed frequently group-oriented.

Intellectual epicenters. One also cannot help but notice the differences between their intellectual epicenters. The intellectual leaders of OD tend to be located in prestigious research universities. The universities where OD took form were MIT and the University of Michigan. Many of the intellectual leaders of OD have been associated with MIT (Beckhard, Schein), Michigan (Likert), Harvard (Argyris, Beer, Walton), Columbia (Burke), and Yale (Alderfer). PP, on the other hand, has its intellectual epicenters at comprehensive and land grant universities. Many of PP's intellectual leaders have been associated with Purdue (McCormick, Viteles), Bowling Green (Guion), Michigan State (Schmitt, Hunter), and Minnesota (Dunnette).

There is probably some relationship between the types of universities that are the intellectual epicenters of PP and OD and the nature of the fields, practitioners, and clients. Major research universities tend to be involved in theory development and the creation of new knowledge, whereas comprehensive and land grant universities are oriented toward application. This may explain, in part, the atheoretical and scientist–practitioner orientation of PP; it may also suggest why OD is less empirical and more theory-based.

Another difference is that professors and students at major research universities are probably oriented towards a top management perspective, more comfortable dealing with the top management, and at ease with activities related to top management skills and functions (e.g., policy making, strategy, impression management, negotiation, and public presentations). Research universities are also more likely to have alumni who move into top management positions.

Upper-level managers appear to be most comfortable with long-term relationships with consultants who serve as sounding boards. They also prefer consultants who deal with process issues. Lower-level managers, on the other hand, seem to be more interested in consultants who can solve immediate, well-defined problems (Gattiker & Larwood, 1985). The students and faculty attracted to comprehensive and land grant universities are probably most comfortable with the technical roles, middle management, and personnel orientation of PP.

CREATING AN ORGANIZATION DEVELOPMENT
OF PERSONNEL PSYCHOLOGY

Why is it important to have an OD perspective of PP? I believe that if PP is not transformed so that it deals with resistance to change, the workgroup, top management concerns, and interpersonal processes—in short, if it does not become integrated with OD—its influence will remain with a small cadre of technicians. On the other hand, if OD it not transformed so that it deals with job analysis, personnel selection, training, and performance appraisal, OD's perceived usefulness to management may wane.

A lack of integration of OD and PP will be a tragedy for PP, OD, and applied behavioral science. More importantly, it will be a tragedy for organizations in the United States which are losing ground in the competitive, global economy. One reason our organizations are losing ground is that they are failing to utilize behavioral science knowledge to select and train workers with the skills to compete in the 21st century (Dertouzos et al., 1989).

PP can help overcome these problems, and it can increase the acceptance and utilization of its techniques by integrating itself with OD. In particular, PP needs to: deal more with organizational context, work with units of analysis that are larger than the individual, focus more on interpersonal behavior and pyschological processes, and acknowledge and deal with resistance to change.

Organizational Context

One way to come closer to an organization development of personnel psychology is to enlarge the context of PP technologies. Traditionally personnel psychologists regarded their techniques as neutral, isolated technologies that could be applied antiseptically to any organization (Colarelli, 1991). However, systems theory tells us otherwise (Colarelli & Stumpf, 1990).

Diagnosing organizational cultures. As integral parts of the systems in which they are embedded, personnel programs *reflect* an organization's culture. Therefore, existing personnel programs can be used as information to diagnose a culture. The way people are selected and the attributes an organization (actually) considers when hiring and promoting people are clues to an organization's value system. So, too, are an organization's performance appraisal and reward systems. What an organization rewards reflects its values. Does its reward system emphasize equity or equality? How comfortable are people in establishing standards, evaluating performance, and making distinctions among people? How does an organization train its employees? Is training carefully thought out and rigorous? If so, this suggests a strong culture and clear values—for training is an important way to socialize newcomers. Or is training confused, sporadic, and mediocre? If so, this suggests a weak culture with confused and vague values.

Integral organizational components. When PP technologies are perceived and implemented as integral components of an organization's culture and strategy, they are less likely to be perceived as tools that management uses to manipulate employees. Rather, employees are more likely to view PP technologies as activities that are good for them and good for the organization. Employees would view PP technologies as athletes view rigorous training exercises. United Parcel Service (UPS), for example, uses time and motion studies—often considered nefarious tools to squeeze productivity out of workers (Baritz, 1960). Although UPS "is run by stopwatches," this approach has "earned the company a consistently high corporate reputation, and its employee turnover rate is only 4 percent" (Moorhead & Griffin, 1989, pp. 126-127). UPS employees do not chafe at time and motion studies because they view them as integral parts of a corporate culture that prides itself on efficiency and hard work—and a culture where employees reap substantial financial rewards from efficiency and hard work.

When managers and personnel psychologists conceptualize PP technologies as parts of a larger system, the technologies are more likely to be infused into the culture, and employees will be less resistant to them. They will have more meaning to employees. When employees accept PP technologies, there will be more commitment to using them, and they will have a greater impact on organizational effectiveness.

Levers for change. Another way that PP technologies can be integrated into the larger organizational context is by using them as levers for organizational change. Schein (1985) points out that leaders shape organizational culture through five mechanisms, four of which are in the domain of PP:

1. what leaders pay attention to, measure, and control (performance appraisal)
2. leader reactions to critical incidents and crises
3. deliberate role modeling, teaching, and coaching (training)
4. criteria for allocation of rewards and status (performance appraisal)
5. criteria for recruitment, selection, promotion, retirement, and excommunication (personnel selection and performance appraisal).

Personnel selection, for example, can have organization-wide effects. In particular, personnel selection can be one of the most effective strategies for organizational change (Schein, 1985; Schneider, 1987). Organizations develop their unique cultures in large measure through the influence of the personalities of the founder and leaders, and because of the type of people who are attracted to and stay in an organization. People self-select into organizations based on the fit between their personalities and the organization's culture (Argyris, 1958; Schein, 1985; Schneider, 1987). When an organization hires people with values similar to its culture, the culture is likely to remain stable. A powerful method for changing an organization's culture, therefore, is to hire people with different values.

Performance appraisal, if viewed within a larger organizational context, is also a lever for organizational change (Mohrmann, Resnick-West, & Lawler, 1989). First, the organization develops its strategy—that is, it determines its priorities and where it wants to go. Second, it identifies the behaviors that people need to perform for the organization to realize its strategy. Third, it appraises employees' behavior, reward behaviors that are in accord with strategy guidelines, and takes note of how employee performance is affecting the system as a whole.

One of the best examples of how performance appraisal (loosely defined) was used to implement policy comes from post-World War II Japan (McCraw, 1986). After the Occupation, Japan's business and government elites determined that Japan should become a world economic power—focusing first on heavy industry and later on knowledge-based technology. To do so required substantial amounts of capital. Japan's elites adopted a pay-as-you-go strategy. To implement this strategy, Japanese structures would be set up to encourage Japanese citizens to save significant portions of their income. To discourage consumer borrowing, interest payments on loans were taxed. To encourage savings, interest earned from savings accounts was not taxed; home buying was discouraged by requiring substantial down payments; and salary increases were given in the form of yearly bonuses. The example is straightforward. Japan's leaders developed a strategic plan. Desired behaviors for the rank and file were identified. Individuals who performed those behaviors were rewarded. And the amount of capital that accumulated in Japan's banks provided the feedback on results.

Focus on Larger Units than the Individual

An OD approach to PP would move the focus to larger units of analysis than the individual—to the workgroup and the organization. While the traditional emphasis of PP on the individual is important, many of PP's activities—selection, appraisal, training—are organizational activities. Thus, the effectiveness of PP techniques may be enhanced by focusing on larger units of analysis.

Consider, for example, personnel selection. Traditionally, personnel selection has been concerned with matching individual skills with job tasks. For example, if a job's primary tasks are typing and filing, a selection specialist would measure applicants' typing and filing skills, and hire those with the highest typing and filing test scores (Dunnette, 1966). More recently, selection has centered on measuring intelligence, assuming that intelligent applicants will perform better than less intelligent applicants on all jobs in all situations (Schmidt & Hunter, 1981). Yet, both of these approaches focus on the individual person and the individual job.

Most people, however, work within a group and within the context of an organization. Sampson (1963, p. 155) points out that a fundamental requirement of individual and collective survival is "the degree of coordination among the actions of two or more persons involved in any particular interaction situation." This coordination requires knowledge about the expected behaviors of others. Thus, a new employee contributes to the survival of the organization not only by performing specific tasks (i.e., formal job requirements), but also by interacting effectively within the workgroup and organization. Thus, a key issue in selection is the compatibility of applicants with the workgroup and organization (Colarelli, 1991; Colarelli & Boos, 1992; Homans, 1974).

Other areas in the selection process also relate to larger units. These include the integration of newcomers into the work group (Mills, 1957); how selection practices influence an organization's adaptation to the environment (Colarelli, 1991); similarities between selection practices and initiation rites (Kamens, 1977); and the relationship between the information generated by selection practices and expectation effects (Eden & Shani, 1982).

Interpersonal Behavior

Almost nothing is written in the PP literature about interpersonal behavior—especially the interpersonal behavior that is involved when applying PP techniques. Many of the techniques and applications of PP could be improved by focusing in greater measure on interpersonal behavior (Argyris, 1958; 1976). The following comment made by Argyris in 1976 is as true today as it was then:

Why is it that industrial psychologists have . . . not manifested the same intensity of research interest in the interpersonal relationships of the situations their technology creates [as they have in their technology]? (Argyris, 1976, p. 158)

There are at least three areas in which increased attention to interpersonal relations could help in testing and selection: civility, explanation, and feedback. These can make selection more appealing. It is important to make the selection situation positive because this is usually applicants' first encounter with the organization. Job applicants may also be potential customers or clients of the organization. If they are offended during the selection process, they may not want to spend their money there as customers or be clients.

Civility. The civility of organizational members during the selection process influences how applicants react to the selection process and perceive the organization (Alderfer & McCord, 1970; Schein, 1972; Taylor & Bergmann, 1987). Interpersonal processes can be enhanced during selection by being polite to applicants and treating them as individuals. The emphasis of testing on standardization, control, security, and mass processing has the effect of reducing people to objects. The testing process does not have to proceed in this fashion. Work is needed on methods to individualize the selection process without loss of test integrity.

Explanation. It is also important to provide applicants with an explanation of what the selection process will involve, why the organization uses specific types of tests or other procedures, and how it makes selection decisions. Applicants can be given a "realistic preview" of the testing process by an interviewer, incumbent, or video tape. The preview would describe the format and purpose of the tests, why tests are used, and how the organization will make selection decisions.

Feedback. After applicants take a test, they should be provided with their test results and an interpretation. With computer technology, it is possible to get this kind of information back to applicants quickly and inexpensively—although some degree of personal counseling should be involved. Feedback provides the applicants with something (self knowledge) even if they don't get the job; it also shows evidence that the organization is concerned about them personally. Applicants who are not hired should also be given information on the standards to qualify for a job.

Treating applicants respectfully benefits the organization and it benefits society. Applicants who are treated respectfully would be less likely to file lawsuits if they were not hired (it is hard to sue someone you like). They should also form a positive impression of the organization—which is good public relations. Society also benefits when organizations give applicants a clear indication of selection standards and feedback on their test performance. This motivates people to improve themselves and raises standards throughout the population (cf. Klitgaard, 1985).

One gets the impression that some OD scholars and practitioners see employee testing as an authoritarian anachronism with little relevance to modern organizations (Schein, 1972). If this is so, then why do the Japanese—whose management skills and economic prowess have become the envy of the industrialized world—test extensively (McCraw, 1986; Sasaki, 1981)? The problem is not with testing. Tests can be a valuable tool to improve productivity. The problem in the United States is with the way that organizations use tests.

Focus on Process

Traditionally, PP has focused on content and measurement, and has ignored psychological processes (Argyris, 1976). I will suggest how an emphasis on process can benefit three PP technologies: job analysis, performance appraisal, and training.

Process in job analysis. Job analysis is the cornerstone of PP technologies (McCormick, 1979). Job analysis is gathering information on jobs, by systematic methods, for a purpose. Levine (1983) goes a step further and suggests that a job analysis should result in breaking a job down into specific tasks and elements.

A problem with job analysis's focus on content and methods is that it presupposes a steady state and an "idealist" reality. Traditional job analysis is based on the assumption that jobs change slowly and that jobs possess a fixed, underlying structure. Therefore, the only way to deal with change is to conduct another job analysis when the job has sufficiently changed to justify another analysis.

Similarly, most discussions of job analysis assume that jobs have an ideal reality. That is, the purpose of analyzing a job is to identify what the job "really" consists of: At the core of every job is an ideal constellation of elements that define the job. The purpose of job analysis, therefore, is to cut through the surface reality to uncover the true, ideal nature of the job. Another view is that reality is socially constructed (Berger & Luckmann, 1967). This view assumes that the nature of a job is neither cast in stone nor made up of fundamental elements. A job is a social role that is constantly negotiated by a *process* of communicating expectations (Kahn, Wolfe, Quinn, Snoek, & Rosenthal, 1964).

Although it is important to systematically gather information on jobs and to be clear about what people should do, a focus on the *process* of job analysis fosters an awareness of the changing nature of jobs, facilitates goal development and clarification, and enhances communication about jobs. The process of job analysis involves written and oral communication about jobs and interaction among individuals who have a stake in a job (cf. Levine, 1983, p. 95). A focus on communication and interaction presupposes that there is some give-and-take among parties, some difference in perspective (or at least an incomplete understanding of the other's perspective), and a negotiated reality. Communication implies sending and receiving expectations and altering expectations. There is more emphasis on the job as a constellation of *roles* (mediated by communication) and less of an emphasis on the job as a constellation of tasks. When job analysis focuses on process, it implicitly acknowledges the fluid nature of jobs.

A focus on process in job analysis can also help develop and clarify goals. Goals are expected future states. Job goals, then, are expectations about what an individual will accomplish on the job. They can be vague ("I will work hard and do a good job") or specific ("I will sell 10 widgets by August 1"). Specific goals are usually better than vague goals. Dialogue or writing helps people clarify goals. Articulating one's ideas and expectations to another, writing them down, and defending them force one to clarify one's thoughts. Moreover, by engaging in dialogue about a job or writing about it, people often become aware of aspects of their jobs about which they previously had only vague ideas.

Dialogue and writing foster clear thinking in three ways. First, they *individuate* vague thoughts (Dewey, 1934/1958). Individuating undifferentiated thought identifies components of ideas and problems, and this makes thinking about them easier and systematic. Second, dialogue and writing *externalize* the internal symbolic models in people's heads (cf. Gilhooly, 1982). And third, dialogue and writing make it easier for thought to be symbolically *manipulated*. When people externalize internal symbolic models, these become more concrete, and, when written down, permanent. It then becomes easier for people to use, manipulate, and revise them. External thought can also be scrutinized and manipulated by others. Thus, externalization—through dialogue and writing—makes thought more accessible and amenable for improvement and clarification. By creating a structure that facilitates dialogue and writing about jobs, job analysis helps individuals achieve greater clarity about what they expect to accomplish.

In addition, the process of job analysis fosters understanding about jobs among people. Traditionally, job analysis procedures involve job incumbents describing their jobs to job analysts (in person or via a questionnaire). However, when *other people* are involved in the process, more people learn about the nature of jobs in the organization. Job analysis questionnaries, for example, can stimulate the sharing of job expectations between, say, a manager and his or her boss. Hemphill (1959) discusses how managers and their bosses can each fill out a job analysis questionnaire on the manager's job—independently indicating the areas they think are most and least important. After filling out the questionnaires, they meet and discuss their responses—noting where they agree and where they disagree. The job analysis questionnaire provides a mechanism for managers and their bosses to discuss and reconcile differences over job priorities. Understanding is also fostered if a job analyst interviews a *group* of employees. By engaging in a group discussion, individuals learn about one another's jobs. In addition, supervisors could ask personnel psychologists to train *employees* to conduct (or help to conduct) job analyses. By being involved in job analyses, employees gain understanding of what others do. Finally, job analysis can facilitate communication when job analysis information is fed back throughout the organization in a process similar to the feedback cascade procedure used with survey feedback.

This suggests that we should not view job analysis as a "one shot" event that only occurs when it is time it design or update a personnel technology. Rather, we should view job analysis as a regular organizational activity—similar to opinion surveys. Organizations should conduct job analyses every two or three years to stimulate communication about jobs, clarify job goals, and foster understanding of what jobs entail.

Process in performance appraisal. Traditional research and practice in performance appraisal has been driven by content and measurement. Performance appraisal research has—for years—focused on identifying performance dimensions and how to measure them (Banks & Murphy, 1985; Bernardin & Beatty, 1983). Performance appraisal systems used to be "left to experts in the backroom. . . . Most of the literature is concerned with the technical details and evaluation of measurement forms" (Mohrmann, Resnick-West, & Lawler, 1989, p. xi).

Mohrmann et al. (1989) argue that organizations can and should use performance appraisal systems for organization change and development. Their approach to performance appraisal entails employee involvement—from the top to the bottom. Their focus is on the design, implementation, and utilization *processes*.

Performance appraisal is usually unpleasant for the appraiser and appraisee, and it involves conflicting goals (Porter, Lawler, & Hackman, 1975). On the one hand, managers need to point out where a subordinate should improve; they also need to curtail rewards to marginal performers. On the other hand, managers want to motivate employees and maintain good working relationships. Subordinates want honest feedback, but they also want to present themselves in the best light. A focus on the process in the appraisal interview—that is, on communication and dialogue—can reduce tension and improve the interpersonal dynamics of the appraisal interview. As a result, understanding increases, and the performance appraisal interview becomes more constructive (Maier, 1958).

A critical issue in performance appraisal relates to *what* should be assessed. In many jobs, the performance dimensions are not cut and dry, and are a negotiated reality. Again, by focusing on dialogue, the performance appraisal interview changes from an adversarial exercise in interpreting forms and arguing about ratings to negotiating a mutually acceptable reality. Not only should this be a more satisfying procedure, but it should also identify realistic areas of performance. This helps both the supervisor and subordinate better understand the nature of the job and each other's constraints and expectations.

Process in training. As with performance appraisal, the bulk of PP research in training has involved content and measurement. The focus has been on training techniques and training evaluation methods (e.g., Goldstein, 1986; Wexley & Latham, 1981). Until recently, little work has discussed the *processes* for developing and implementing training programs. Robinson and Robinson's (1989) book is an exception. It discusses the importance of developing a partnership with management, sharing responsibility, managing projects, and working with management to identify training needs and to determine if training is a solution to perceived problems.

They argue that although personnel and human resource development (HRD) professionals have been delivering training programs for years, the measure of success was quantity—how many training programs were delivered. They call this *training for activity.* In training for activity, management holds the HR department accountable for activity, not results; further, management assumes no responsibility for training.

The alternative is *training for impact.* Critical to this is the creation of a strategic partnership with management. A strategic partnership with management involves includes two processes: (1) forming collaborative relationships with clients (managers), and (2) identifying business needs and aligning training with those needs. To successfully identify business and training needs, HRD professionals must interact with management. Training specialists cannot adequately identify business and training needs just by passing out questionnaires. If training is to be successful, personnel professionals also must work collaboratively with management throughout all of the phases of training—from identifying needs and planning through implementation and evaluation. Collaboration means that the personnel professional forms a partnership with management in which management assumes equal responsibility for training. For this to work, personnel professionals must establish a close, ongoing relationship with managers.

PP's emphasis on content and methods, its lack of attention to the larger context in which training occurs, and personnel psychologists' lack of familiarity and comfort with managers—especially top managers—have contributed to the training for activity trap in which they have been enmeshed for years. However, by emphasizing the process between personnel psychologists and managers, training can become more effective and results-oriented.

Resistance to Change

Change and resistance to change in personnel systems are critical areas where work is needed. OD has barely touched change and implementation in PP technologies. And PP has not moved forward in these areas. Yet, as anyone who has implemented a selection, training, or performance appraisal system knows, it not the mechanistic equivalent of putting in a new set of spark plugs in a car. People—unless they have a good reason not to—tend to resist change, and this includes change in personnel systems. In fact, changes in personnel systems may be among the areas that generate the most resistance because they impinge upon important rewards (who gets a job, who gets rewarded, and how much).

A good paradigm for dealing with resistance to change with PP technologies is Maier's (1963) quality and acceptance paradigm. He suggests that the quality of a group decision is the product of the quality of the decision *and* its acceptance. The issue of acceptance is critical because even brilliant ideas will not be implemented unless they are accepted by the people who are affected by them. The key to effective acceptance and implementation of PP technologies, therefore, is employee involvement. This suggests that PP's obsession with technical standards might be overemphasized when dealing with the realities of resistance to change and implementation. Involving organizational members at all levels in design and implementation may sacrifice some rigor, but the rigor that is lost will more than be made up in the lowering of resistance and a more successful implementation.

SUGGESTIONS AND A PROGNOSIS
FOR AN ORGANIZATION DEVELOPMENT
OF PERSONNEL PSYCHOLOGY

What are the prospects that OD will become integrated into the theory and practice of PP? This is likely to happen, although not quickly, because of pressure from the environment. The change process may follow a path like this: environmental pressure → changes in practioners' behavior → changes in academic research and writing → continued changes in practitioner behavior.

The pressures from the environment that are likely to increase integration between OD and PP include: the global economy, competition from the Pacific Rim and Europe, the increasing sophistication of consumers, and the increased technical sophistication required for jobs. Skilled human resources are a key problem in the United States' ability to compete in the global economy (Dertouzos et al., 1989). Incompetent and poorly trained workers are now an impediment to the United States regaining its position of economic leadership. More and more, American companies are realizing that—like the Japanese and Germans who have surpassed them—they must take employee selection and training seriously. Therefore, more attention will have to be paid to the processes of change and implementation—that is to the OD aspects of PP.

These environmental pressures will in turn force PP practitioners to be more sensitive to change and implementation issues: Managers will want more than a technical report or a quick-fix technique. They will want state-of-the-art selection and training programs that are effectively implemented throughout their organizations. Paradigms for effective change and implementation of personnel programs are likely to come first in books written by practitioners who integrate theory with their own experiences in implementing personnel programs (e.g., Byham, 1989; Robinson & Robinson, 1989).

Environmental pressures, new activities by practitioners, and books by consultants should stimulate academics to pursue the organization development of personnel psychology. In addition to research and wiring, integration between PP and OD may occur in other ways in universities. Scholars might alter their own selection procedures to blend the two fields. For example, in the selection of graduate students, programs that have a strong PP emphasis may admit more students who have humanities backgrounds. Programs with an OD emphasis might want to admit more graduate students who have quantitative backgrounds. Courses that integrate concepts from both fields would be helpful. They might approach the technical and implementation issues of PP and OD technologies from the perspectives of each field. One way to teach such a course would be to have it team-taught, with one professor an OD specialist and the other a PP specialist. Other OD–PP hybrids likewise will be welcome.

The integration of OD and PP will occur slowly, but—given the changes in the environment—it will be inevitable. Hopefully, both academics and practitioners will see the usefulness of a closer link between the two fields, and will therefore speed up the process.

REFERENCES

Alderfer, C. P., & McCord, C. (1970). Personal and situational factors in the recruitment interview. *Journal of Applied Psychology, 54*, 377–385.

Argyris, C. (1958). Some problems in conceptualizing organizational climate: A case study of a bank. *Administrative Science Quarterly, 2*, 501–520.

Argyris, C. (1976). Problems and new directions for industrial psychology. In M. D. Dunnette (Ed.), *Handbook of industrial and organizational psychology* (pp. 151–184). Chicago: Rand McNally.

Arvey, R. D. (1979). *Fairness in selecting employees.* Reading, MA: Addison-Wesley.

Banks, C. G., & Murphy, K. R. (1985). Toward narrowing the research-practice gap in performance appraisal. *Personnel Psychology, 38*, 335–345.

Baritz, L. (1960). *The servants of power.* Middleton, CT: Wesleyan University Press.

Beckhard, R. (1969). *Organization development: Strategies and models.* Reading, MA: Addison-Wesley.

Beer, M. (1980). *Organization change and development.* Santa Monica, CA: Goodyear.

Beer, M., & Walton, A. E. (1987). Organization development and change. In M. R. Rosenzweig & L. W. Porter (Eds.), *Annual review of psychology* (Vol. *38*, pp. 339–367). Palo Alto, CA: Annual Reviews.

Berger, P. L., & Luckmann, T. (1967). *The social construction of reality.* New York: Anchor.

Bernardin, H. J., & Beatty, R. W. (1983). *Performance appraisal: Assessing human behavior at work*. Boston: Kent.

Burke, W. W. (1982). *Organization development*. Boston: Little, Brown.

Byham, W. C. (1989). *Zapp! The lightning of empowerment*. San Diego, CA: University Associates.

Colarelli, S. M. (1991). *The context of hiring practices*. Manuscript submitted for publication.

Colarelli, S. M., & Boos, A. L. (1992). Sociometric and ability-based assignment to work groups: Some implications for personnel selection. *Journal of Organizational Behavior, 13*, 187–196.

Colarelli, S. M., & Stumpf, S. A. (1990). Compatibility and conflict among outcomes of organizational entry strategies: Mechanistic and social systems perspectives. *Behavioral Science, 35*, 1–10.

Dertouzos, M. L., Lestor, R. K., & Solow R. M. (1989). *Made in America: Regaining the productive edge*. Cambridge, MA: MIT Press.

Dewey, J. (1958). *Art as experience*. New York: Capricorn. (Original work published 1934)

Dunnette, M. D. (1966). *Personnel selection and placement*. Monterey, CA: Brooks/Cole.

Dunnette, M. D. (1976). Aptitudes, abilities, and skills. In M. D. Dunnette (Ed.), *Handbook of industrial and organizational psychology* (pp. 473–520). Chicago: Rand McNally.

Eden, D. (1986). OD and self-fulfilling prophecy: Boosting productivity by raising expectations. *Journal of Applied Behavioral Science, 22*, 1–13.

Eden, D., & Shani, A. B., (1982). Pygmalion goes to boot camp: Expectancy, leadership, and trainee performance. *Journal of Applied Psychology, 67, 194–199.*

French, W. L., & Bell, C. H., Jr. (1984). *Organization development*. Englewood Cliffs, NJ: Prentice-Hall.

Gattiker, U. E., & Larwood, L. (1985). Why do clients employ management consultants? *Consultation, 4*, 119–129.

Gilhooly, K. J. (1982). *Thinking*. London: Academic Press.

Goldstein, I. L. (1986). *Training in organizations: Needs assessment, development, and evaluation* (2nd ed.). Monterey, CA: Brooks/Cole.

Greiner, L. E., & Schein, V. E. (1988). *Power and organization development*. Reading, MA: Addison-Wesley.

Hemphill, J. K. (1959, Sept.–Oct.). Job descriptions for executives. *Harvard Business Review*, 55–67.

Homans, G. C. (1974). *Social behavior* (rev. ed.). New York: Harcourt Brace Jovanovich.

Kahn, R. L. Wolfe, D. M., Quinn, R. P., Snoek, J. D., & Rosenthal, R. A. (1964). *Organizational stress: Studies in role conflict and ambiguity*. New York: Wiley.

Kamens, D. H. (1977). Legitimating myths and educational organization: The relationship between organizational ideology and formal structure. *American Sociological Review, 42*, 208–219.

Klitgaard, R. (1985). *Choosing elites*. New York: Basic Books.

Latham. (1988). Human resource training and development. In M. R. Rosenzweig & L. W. Porter (Eds.), *Annual review of psychology* (Vol. 39,
pp. 545–582). Palo Alto, CA: Annual Reviews.

Ledvinka, J., & Scarpello, V. G. (1991). *Federal regulation of personnel
and human resource management.* Boston: PWS-Kent.

Levine, E. L. (1983). *Everything you always wanted to know about job
analysis.* Tampa, FL: Author.

Levitt, T. (1968, March–April). Why business always loses. *Harvard Business Review,* pp. 81–89.

Lewin, K. (1935). *A dynamic theory of personality.* New York: McGraw-Hill.

Lewin, K., Lippitt, R., & White, R. K. (1939). Patterns of aggressive behavior
in experimentally created "social climates." *Journal of Social Psychology, 10,* 271–299.

London, M., & Moses, J. L. (1990). The changing roles of the industrial/
organizational psychologist: From analyst/technician to change agent/
strategist. *The Industrial and Organizational Psychologist, 27,*
17–26.

Maier, N. R. F. (1958). *The appraisal interview.* New York: Wiley.

Maier, N. R. F. (1963). *Problem-solving discussion and conferences.* New
York: McGraw-Hill.

Marrow, A. J. (1969). *The practical theorist: The life and work of Kurt
Lewin.* New York: Basic Books.

McCormick, E. J. (1979) *Job analysis.* New York: AMACOM.

McCraw, T. K. (1986). From partners to competitors: An overview of the
period since World War II. In T. K. McCraw (Ed.), *America versus
Japan* (pp. 1–33). Boston: Harvard Business School Press.

Mills, T. M. (1957). Group structure and the newcomer: An experimental
study of group expansion. Reprinted in R. J. Ofshe (Ed.), *Interpersonal behavior in small groups* (1973: 260–276). Englewood Cliffs,
NJ: Prentice-Hall.

Mohrmann, A. M., Jr., Resnick-West, S. M, & Lawler, E. E. (1989). *Designing performance appraisal systems.* San Francisco: Jossey-Bass.

Moorhead, G., & Griffen R. W. (1989). *Organizational behavior* (2nd ed.).
Boston: Houghton-Mifflin.

Morgan, G. (1986). *Images of organization.* Newbury Park, CA: Sage.

Moskowitz, M. J. (1977). Hugo Munsterberg: A study in the history of
applied psychology. *American Psychologist, 32,* 824–842.

Porter, L. W., Lawler, E. E., & Hackman, J. R. (1975). *Behavior in organizations.* New York: McGraw-Hill.

Robinson, D. G., & Robinson, J. C. (1989). *Training for impact.* San Francisco: Jossey-Bass.

Roethlisberger, F. J., & Dickson, W. J. (1939). *Management and the worker.* Cambridge, MA: Harvard University Press.

Sampson, E. E., (1963). Status congruence and cognitive consistency.
Sociometry, 26, 146–162.

Sasaki, N. (1981). *Management and industrial structure in Japan.* Oxford:
Pergamon Press.

Schein, E. H. (1969). *Process consultation.* Reading, MA: Addison-Wesley.

Schein, E. H. (1972). *Organizational psychology* (2nd ed.). Englewood Cliffs, NJ: Prentice-Hall.

Schein, E. H. (1985). *Organizational culture and leadership.* San Francisco: Jossey-Bass.

Schmidt, F. L., & Hunter, J. E. (1981). Employment testing: Old theories and new research findings. *American Psychologist, 36,* 1128–1137.

Schneider, B. (1987). The people make the place. *Personnel Psychology, 40,* 437–453.

Society for Industrial and Organizational Psychology. (1985). *Guidelines for education and training at the doctoral level in industrial/ organizational psychology.* College Park, MD: Author.

Taylor, F. W. (1911). *Principles of scientific management.* New York: Harper and Row.

Taylor, M. S., & Bergmann, T. J. (1987). Organizational recruitment activities and applicants' reactions at different stages of the recruitment process. *Personnel Psychology, 40,* 261–285.

Tichy, N. M. (1974). Agents of planned social change: Congruence of values, cognitions, and actions. *Administrative Science Quarterly, 19,* 164–182.

Toulmin, S. (1990, June 28). A question of character. *New York Review of Books,* pp. 48–52.

Wexley, K. N., & Latham, G. P. (1981). *Developing and training human resources in organizations.* Glenview, IL: Scott, Foresman.

3

Issues on the Frontier of Organization Development*

William Gellermann
New York, NY

The theme of this book, advances in OD, tends to suggest advances attributable to changes in the practice of OD professionals. This chapter describes several such advances based on the experience I have had since 1981 when I undertook to coordinate a process for developing "A Statement of Values and Ethics By Professionals in Organization and Human Systems Development" (hereafter referred to as "the Statement"). More importantly, that experience has enhanced my consciousness of a different kind of fundamental advance, namely an emerging transformation in the practice of OD attributable to *a change in our collective self-concept and our associated way of being.* Among other things, the following discussion suggests that we are moving from conceiving ourselves as a *collection of independent professionals* to conceiving ourselves as a *community of interdependent professionals.* More specifically, our community is:

* expanding to include all Human Systems Development (HSD) professionals—whose practice encompasses individuals, fami-

---

*This chapter was written from the perspective of my membership in the OD-HSD profession and is addressed to other members of the profession, since the issues are most meaningfully framed and discussed in such a context. By doing this I do not mean to exclude readers who are not OD-HSD professionals. Quite the contrary, I invite them to listen to our dialogue.

All references to the Statement are to "An Annotated Statement of Values and Ethics By Professionals in Organization and Human Systems Development" (Gellermann, Frankel, & Ladenson, 1990). That Statement has been in process of development since 1981, with participation by more than 500 professionals from more than 22 different countries (most recently the USSR and Finland).

lies, industries, communities, societies, and transnational systems—as well as OD professionals[1]

- coordinating its professional practice by means of shared consciousness of a common purpose, vision, values, and ethics[2]
- including within its collective consciousness awareness of its own existence as a subsystem of the more inclusive system of all life on earth.

And a further advance—or at least a potential advance in our communal self-concept implicit in this last item—is of ourselves as a community capable of facilitating the emergence of a global community whose life is coordinated by shared consciousness of a common purpose, vision, values, and ethics. With that advance in our practice, we can expect a vast increase in the synergy available to us, although for many of us the actual change in our practice will probably involve only a slight shift in orientation. However, that shift will alert us to opportunities to contribute to serving our common purpose so when they present themselves, we will be ready, willing, and able to take advantage of them. As more and more of us make that shift, we can expect both our synergy and our collective achievement to increase exponentially.

---

[1] As noted in Gellermann et al. (1990), there are no simple, clear-cut answers to the questions, How inclusive is the OD-HSD community? and Who are its members? But we can identify some of the primary characteristics of the community. "It is an open system composed of people who (1) regard themselves as professionals (they provide service as a means of earning income and not just for the fun of it), (2) share a holistic, systemic perspective in their work (they recognize systems, subsystems, and macrosystems and their interdependencies), (3) possess a professional level of competence (including ethical competence), (4) share the entire system of related beliefs, values, and ethics generally accepted as primary by OD-HSD professionals (which are gradually being made explicit in the Statement), and (5) choose to consider themselves OD-HSD professionals by freely aligning themselves with the purpose and vision that are at the core of their professional community's identity." Furthermore, as the book also says, "Given the OD-HSD context, we can say that all professionals who work with or in relation to human systems—including organization behavior and organization development theorists, researchers, and academics; management development specialists; human resource developers and planners; industrial/ organizational psychologists; and managers—are HSD professionals if they meet the criteria just specified. Of particular importance among those criteria is that they use 'a holistic, systemic perspective in their work'."

[2] Concepts of the profession's purpose, vision, values and ethics are discussed more fully in Gellermann et al. (1990). For the purpose of this chapter, however, it is important to note that as the terms are used here, "values" refers to standards of *importance* (goodness, rightness, desirability, etc.) and "ethics" refers to standards of *behavior* based on values.

This discussion is based on a chapter, "Looking Ahead: Frontier Issues for Human Systems Development Professionals," in a book on the values and ethics of the OD-HSD profession.[3] That original discussion has been expanded upon by this introductory section, the concluding Addenda, and footnotes.

OD-HSD AS A GLOBAL PROFESSIONAL COMMUNITY

Are We a "Profession"? Do We Want to Become One? If So, What Kind?

OD-HSD scholars and practitioners tend to assume that OD-HSD is a profession, or at least that it is well along the way to becoming one. This assumption is based in part on the results of a survey in mid-1989 that suggested that many practitioners think of OD as a profession and consider themselves professionals [see Gellermann et al., 1990].

However, some people, including Peter Block, an outstanding speaker and writer on the practice of OD, have raised questions about the desirability of becoming a profession. (Note: Block did this in personal conversation about a draft of an article written for the *OD Practitioner* [Gellermann, 1990].) Block sees common purpose and vision as primary. His concern is that in institutionalizing ourselves as a profession we could destroy our ability to serve our purpose because institutionalization tends to mean such things as setting boundaries and standards and concentrating on public relations. Those functions could become primary for "the profession" and self-defeating for our common purpose, particularly by excluding outsiders. Function rather than purpose could become primary.

Block said, "Dialogue is the solution because there is no answer." I asked, "But what is the question?" And he said that he thinks dialogue about purpose is the answer to an ethical existence. I asked if that meant he thought dialogue about values and ethics was inappropriate. He said, "No. Dialogue about values and ethics is important, but it requires a context of common purpose to give it meaning." He said, "What we are seeking is some vehicle for social action and service—a vehicle for volunteerism." He stressed that we

---

[3] Adapted from Gellermann, W., Frankel, M.S., & Ladenson, (1990). *Values and ethics in organization and human systems development: Responding to dilemmas in professional life.* San Francisco: Jossey-Bass, pp. 326–362. Used by permission of the publisher.

need to make it easier to help people *in* rather than to keep them *out*. He concluded that what we need has something to do with our spirit.

All those ideas seem reasonable, except for the initial assertion that we are not a profession and should not become one. On first thought, it seems clear that we are in the process of becoming a profession whether we like it or not, and the question is what kind of a profession do we want to be? I agree that dialogue is the solution and that there is no "answer." As I see it, we are involved in a continuing quest for good life, and the lives we live as professionals, individually and collectively, are a continuing answer to that quest; hence no single "answer," but rather a *continuing lived answer*.

In that connection, *I think it is useful for us to live as a professional community—a community whose members are bonded together by a common purpose (an expression of the spirit of our community) and within which we reflect on how we are living our quest.* In particular, we need dialogue about what we want our lives to be (our common quest, our common purpose and vision), what's currently going on (current reality), what we can do as next steps in moving from where we are to where we want to be (action plans), and, particularly, the standards of importance (values) and standards of behavior (ethics) we choose to guide us along the way.

There seems to be general agreement on the importance of a common purpose for our community. As expressed in the Statement; it is "*to promote a widely shared learning and discovery process dedicated to the vision of people living meaningful, productive, good lives in ways that simultaneously serve them, their organizations, their societies, and the world.*"

If we can establish substantial consensus on that or on some other common purpose, we will have taken a major step toward establishing ourselves as a *community* of professionals. In fact, we may be able to avoid the problems Block cites by thinking of ourselves as a "professional community" rather than as a "profession." However, a better solution to those problems may be to see ourselves as a profession—most OD-HSD practitioners seem to think that way anyway, and both the Statement and later sections in this discussion refer to us as a profession—but to be clear that for us *profession means community*. In contrast, we also need to be clear that being a profession does not mean the emphasis on functions (boundary setting and public relations) and the kinds of institutions (organizations, associations, and so on) associated with such other professions as medicine and law. If we can be clear about that, perhaps we can avoid the traps associated with becoming institutionalized. In fact, our best protections from falling into those traps are the consciousness of process and ability to communicate about process that are so important to the work we do with our clients.

Who are "We"?

The current Statement refers to us as "a global professional community." For those professionals who have met one another at international conferences it is gradually becoming clear that "we" are, in fact, *global, professional,* and *a community.* That sense of community is still emerging, and for many of us it has just barely begun, but it seems a logical (as well as a psychological) next step in our own development as a human system.

Our profession began as a scattering of individual practitioners who worked almost exclusively as internal consultants to organizations. We then expanded to include external OD consultants who were generally independent and to some extent competitive. This combined group of internal and external OD consultants met annually at conferences of the U.S. OD Network, the OD Division of the American Society for Training and Development, the OD Institute, the Gesellschaft für Organisationsentwicklung (German-speaking consultants), Division 14 of the American Psychological Association, and several other national groups. Other regional groupings of consultants—national, subnational, and in certain large cities—began to emerge in the United States and other parts of the world. At the same time, teachers from colleges and universities began to emerge in professional groupings, such as the Academy of Management's Organization Development and Organizational Behavior Divisions and the Organizational Behavior Teaching Society.

Eventually the people in these various groupings began seeing themselves as a "profession" that needed to do the things required for really becoming a profession. These necessary steps included establishing a widely shared body of knowledge, clarifying professional competencies, and agreeing on ethical standards, all of which are currently in progress. Though the annual professional meetings were initially national, beginning in the United States and then in such countries as South Africa and Mexico, they have now become multinational—including Europe, Central and South America, the Western Hemisphere, and Southeast Asia, among other regions—and transnational—including gatherings of professionals from countries all around the world, such as the annual meetings of the OD Institute and the International OD Association.

The profession seems to be on the verge of transformation from a worldwide network of independent individual practitioners to a global community of interdependent professionals who, by virtue of their competence and their consciousness, will be able to take on challenges that would have been inconceivable as long as they viewed themselves primarily as individuals.

Is It Possible to Develop General Agreement on Values and Ethics Among OD-HSD Professionals Throughout the World, Particularly Given the Fact of Major Cultural Differences?

Geert Hofstede (1980) has reported the results of a study of 116,000 employees of a single, multinational corporation in 40 countries around the world. Based on statistical analysis of the data, he identified four primary dimensions that he used to describe and differentiate the cultures of those forty countries. They are *Power Distance* (the degree to which unequal distribution of power in institutions and organizations is accepted); *Uncertainty Avoidance* (the degree to which uncertain, ambiguous situations are threatening and people seek to avoid them); *Individualism-Collectivism* (the degree to which people are expected to take care of themselves and their immediate family or, at the collective extreme, they expect their relatives, clan, organization, or other in-group to care for them in exchange for absolute loyalty to the group); and *Masculinity* (the degree to which people hold masculine values, such as assertiveness and acquisition of money and things, and lack of concern for people and the quality of their lives).

In spite of methodological criticism of his study (Goodstein & Hunt, 1981; Hofstede, 1981), Hofstede's results clearly suggest that substantial cultural differences exist along the four dimensions he identified. And, more important for our discussion, his results indicate that certain values that seem central to OD-HSD may be more reflections of the U.S. culture that gave birth to the field than they are a sound basis for establishing a global perspective for the field's values and ethics.

Two alternatives for dealing with cultural differences in developing professional ethics on a global scale seem reasonable. The first can be called the *pluralist alternative:* that is, one in which countries or clusters of countries with similar cultures develop common statements. Ideally all of those statements would follow a similar format so that similarities and differences could be readily identified. The second alternative can be called the *universalist alternative:* that is, one in which a substantial consensus is developed around a single common statement throughout OD-HSD's global professional community, but with recognition of and allowances for cultural differences.

The way the second alternative might come about can be illustrated by the contrast between the primary "I" consciousness of individualistic cultures and the primary "we" consciousness of collectivist cultures. OD-HSD tends to transcend that apparent conflict by viewing it not as "*either* I *or* we" but as "*both* I *and* we." And within the "both-and" perspective, the orientation is to find or create whole-win solutions that coordinate serving the good of the individual and the collective, rather than subordinating one to the other.

By choosing the "both I and we" orientation toward who we are, we transcend the apparent polarity of individualism and collectivism and acknowledge the possibility that individual uniqueness can be enhanced by membership in the collective. We are not required to make that choice, but freedom allows us to make it. I believe that such a choice is particularly necessary for members of the OD-HSD profession in order to realize our highest potential, as individuals and as a professional community. For example, it is possible for us to think of ourselves as:

- Persons first, then members of our national professional communities, and, finally, members of our global professional community
- Members of the global OD-HSD professional community first, then members of our national professional communities, and, finally, persons
- Persons first, then members of the global OD-HSD professional community, and, finally, members of our national professional communities

For me, the third alternative, which focuses first on personal identity, then on global identity, and finally on national identity, is preferable. (This preference, however, may reflect my development within the conditions of U.S. culture.) In any case, it is important to understand that by personal identity I include that which some people call "higher self." In other words, it is that which is at the core of personal integrity. I believe that if we all ground ourselves in such a personal identity, we root ourselves in the common ground of all human life. I do not know exactly what it means to "root ourselves in the common ground," but I believe the OD-HSD profession is particularly well qualified to facilitate a widely shared learning and discovery process that seeks to establish such meaning.

The belief that there is a ground common to all human life is especially important when we practice in cultures other than the one(s) within which we were raised. Cultural relativism tends to treat all cultures as equally "right" and to require outsiders to live within the constraints of the cultures where they live. One of our colleagues, an American who has practiced in the Far East, expressed his difficulty with cultural relativism in these words: "If I live in [another country], should I be a cultural prisoner—an alien forever . . . a socially neutered respectful observer? I believe I am a World citizen with the right to express myself on any issue anywhere." Relativism certainly offers pragmatic guidance on how to act, but it is not necessarily *right* if we accept the idea of a ground common to all human life. As just noted, the OD-HSD profession has unique contributions to make in the quest for such common ground, which is, in my judgment, primary in our collective "quest for a good life."

In any case, we can expect the discovery or creation of our global professional community to be an exciting process. We can undertake it as a contribution by our profession not only to our own development but also to global peace and to the constructive resolution of differences throughout the world.

OD-HSD COMMUNITY AS SERVANT
TO THE WHOLE SYSTEM OF LIFE ON EARTH

Who Is Our Client? To Whom Are We Responsible and For What?

Though these questions have been in the consciousness of Organization Development professionals for a long time, they take on new significance as the profession expands its scope to encompass all human systems. This issue was raised in a note criticizing an earlier version of the Statement: "The whole Statement is written as though 'the client' is the organization or system as a whole. In fact, there is always a particular client within the system—the head of the outfit, the board of directors, or the director of personnel. An ethic of consulting must deal with that special relationship. . . . It's important to think through the balance between working for one's particular client and for the system as a whole."

There is an apparent paradox in that criticism. Usually individuals and occasionally groups employ our services, and we are accountable to them as well as having an ethical obligation to them. At the same time, we commit ourselves to "serve the long-term well-being of our client systems and their stakeholders" (Guideline III-A in the Statement.). Our specific ethical obligation to those who employ us is somewhat ambiguous in the Statement because its reference to "client" can be read as referring to those who employ us or the system or both. That ambiguity is intentional since our mission involves serving both. Serving our employers' special interests is both practical and ethical—practical in that we cannot continue to serve a system without serving our employer's interests, and ethical in that when we contract with an employer we are ethically bound to fulfill that contract. But we need to be careful that in acting under that contract we do not do things prohibited by our ethics, including acts that would harm the system.

Answering the question "Who is our client?" requires a broader perspective than one focused only on the person(s) with whom we contract. We are *system* development consultants and *the system is our client.* In the same way that physicians serve the health of their patients and do not limit themselves to responding only to what the patients want them to do, we have a broader responsibility. To the extent we realistically can, we have an ethical responsibility to serve the long-term, interdependent interests of the system and its stakeholders, as noted in the preceding paragraph. If the special interests of those who employ us conflict seriously with those of the whole system or any of its stakeholders, we are faced with a dilemma; the Statement gives some guidance, as in Guideline III-D, regarding conflicts of interest. Again, though, such dilemmas involve considerations that are both practical (doing what it takes to continue serving the system) and ethical (doing things that are consistent with serving our employer, the whole system, and its stakeholders).

The Statement acknowledges that we "accept differences in the expectations and interests of different stakeholders and realize that those differences cannot be reconciled all the time" (Guideline III-D-4). That gives us some room for making the practical adjustments necessary to serve those who employ us. However, we are also accountable to our consciences and we have a duty to our profession, whose ethics focus on the good of our client systems and all their stakeholders. And, finally, it is important to recognize that many of us believe that ultimately our client is the world.

To What Extent Do the Aspirations of OD-HSD Professionals Include Serving "the Well-Being of All Life on Earth"?

A questionnaire survey in 1983 asked about "helping organizations align their purposes with the welfare of the earth and all its people"

(Gellermann, 1984). Responses were strong and varied widely, ranging from "I like the idealism there. Who knows where the aim for the stars will take us?" and "Yes. Definitely," to "Pretentious and irrelevant do-goodism," "Come on! I for one have no messianic complex," and "too grandiose." In addition, others noted that we have a responsibility to serve all life and not just human life, so the Statement was changed to read, both more simply and more comprehensively, "the well-being of all life on earth."

The issue is still open. The primary question seems to be: Does OD-HSD as a profession have a global aspiration? In view of the fact that we work with human systems, we are working with open systems and they are, therefore, ultimately subsystems within the global human system. Therefore it can be argued that a global perspective is essential, even from the limited point of view of our clients' interests. Although our organizational clients may not see the connection, it is appropriate for us to take a leadership role in relating the organization's interests to those of the global system whenever we can do so effectively. This does not mean, though, that it is necessary to stress that connection with all clients under all conditions. However, it is important to recognize that OD-HSD professionals are uniquely qualified, by virtue of their membership in a global professional community, to maintain a global perspective and assert it whenever it might make a positive difference.

Can the OD-HSD Profession-As-A-Whole Contribute to Developing the Whole System Composed of All Human Life on Earth?[4]

This issue is similar to but different from the issue just discussed about the extent to which we aspire to serving "the well-being of all life on earth." That issue focused primarily on our relationship with our client organizations and other human systems, by putting our service to them in the context of whether that service is good for "the well-being of all life on earth." In contrast, this issue focuses on all life on earth *as a human system* and suggests that the OD-HSD profession as a whole has the potential for facilitating the develop-

---

[4] This section raises a question that deserves attention, namely are "all human life on earth" and "all life on earth" the same thing? Some contend not, based on the belief that not all life meets the criterion of being human, namely "life conscious of itself." Others, such as Peter Russell in *The Global Brain* (1983), see them as similar, since they conceive of a consciousness that transcends the consciousness of individual human beings.

ment of that system in a manner analogous to the service OD professionals give to their organizational clients.

The OD-HSD profession has the potential for becoming a significant subsystem within the macrosystem comprised of all human life on earth. If the profession will develop itself as a global professional community and apply to itself the kinds of developmental approaches it encourages its clients to use, it seems reasonable to conclude that it can contribute to improving the quality of all human life by improving that life's ability to function as a human system. Among other things, this will involve supporting the creation of a global vision, with which some professionals are already involved, through a project called "Global Cooperation for a Better World," headed by the wife of the secretary general of the United Nations, Mrs. Marcela Perez de Cuellar. It is also likely to include, among other contributions, ways of helping our clients throughout the world in:

- Clarifying their values and ethics in ways compatible with achieving and maintaining a sustainable global society
- Enhancing whole-win, cooperative aspects of their cultures
- Increasing their ability to function democratically both internally and externally, enabling the members of their client systems to participate in making decisions about system functioning, on the one hand, and enabling the client systems to participate in decisions by the more inclusive systems of which they are members, on the other

In doing this, cultural differences will need to be acknowledged and honored to as great an extent as possible. In cases of conflict, however, OD-HSD professionals will ideally guide their action by asking, "Is it good for the world?"

PROACTIVELY MONITORING ENTRY INTO AND PRACTICE OF THEIR PROFESSION BY MEMBERS OF THE OD-HSD COMMUNITY

To What Extent, If Any, is the Profession Responsible for Monitoring Entry to the Profession and the Practice of its Members?

Monitoring practice and practitioners has been identified as one of the primary elements in the emergence of a full-fledged profession. However, there has been opposition among OD-HSD practitioners to our becoming a profession because of the possibility that we could become a regulatory clique that controls entry and practice as have other, more well-established professions such as medicine and law. That opposition is based in part on grounds that we may overly institutionalize and rigidify ourselves. There are also concerns that we could become monopolistic and exploitative, as Shepard (1983) noted in describing the typical evolutionary pattern of professions. It is important that we acknowledge those possibilities and, at the same time, be clear that we can develop ways of avoiding them *if we choose to do so.*

As societies become more dependent on professional services, it is vital that professions and professionals be held accountable for their conduct and for their commitment to public service in exchange for the public's trust. However law is a severely limited social tool because it tends to focus on prohibiting socially harmful behavior and is relatively ineffective in encouraging behavior that serves the common good. The more the professions can monitor themselves in preventing harm and encouraging their members to serve the common good, the less society needs to intervene. And the more individuals can monitor themselves, the less their profession needs to intervene.

But it seems clear the OD-HSD profession-as-a-whole will have to act in the not-too-distant future; its primary choice is whether to proact or react. Some may prefer to finesse the issues by acting as if we have no collective responsibility, but I find that position literally irresponsible and, therefore, unacceptable. In my judgment, we cannot afford much longer to ignore the issues of monitoring entry and practice or to treat them as if they are of low priority. My preference is to anticipate probable difficulties, prepare for them, and then revise our preparations based on our experience, rather than wait for difficulties to arise and then react to them.

We have already touched on the issue of monitoring entry. I agree with Hinckley (1986) that our profession, by definition, should be as inclusive as possible. But that does not mean ignoring the issue of inclusion. Most of us, I think, prefer to emphasize establishing ways of measuring or otherwise identifying the competencies by which people can qualify as "professional" and then making the necessary learning experiences available for all those who want to become professionals. A number of efforts are already under way for doing both of these things (for example, see Gellermann et al., 1990).

Many professionals have taken individual responsibility for monitoring their own practice by means of a peer review process. Some professional associations have established criteria for membership, including Association for Creative Change (ACC), which includes participation in its peer review process as its primary criterion. In this connection, the demise of Certified Consultants International (CCI), suggests that support for voluntary peer review is relatively weak. To my knowledge there is no comprehensive, profession-wide effort underway to provide for periodic reviews of our practice and our competence so that we can assure ourselves that as a profession we are maintaining ourselves at a professional level.

In my opinion, we have a collective responsibility to the public we serve to review our practice and our competence, although we may be reluctant to do so individually. Initiating such an effort is a primary responsibility of those with leadership power within existing professional associations. At the same time, I also acknowledge that those "leaders" can lead only where their members are willing to follow. I am convinced that what I am suggesting will not happen until a significant number of influential people ask for collective action toward creating a process for periodic review of our profession. I do not know what that process would look like, but I am confident that collectively we can design something that will work for us. As I see it, we need to use our individual freedom responsibly to create a system that enhances our ability to work collectively. It will mean that we give up some of our independence, which some of us are understandably reluctant to do, but, for me, that is the essence of maturing into interdependence. I particularly want to call on people throughout the global OD-HSD community to use their influence in creating a professionwide effort by, among other things, asking the leadership groups of their national or multinational associations to inform their members of the need for co-creating some means of periodic review of the "health" of our profession and enrolling them in the co-creation process. (The remainder of this section discusses professional structures that might make such review possible.)

In discussing the status of OD as a profession, White and Wooten (1986, p. 193) quote the Society of Personnel Administration's definition of a professional as "a person who is in an occupation requiring a high level of training and proficiency. This person has high standards of achievement with respect to acquiring unique knowledge and skills. A person who is committed to continued study, growth, and improvement for the purpose of rendering the most effective public service. This level of training, proficiency, and ethical standards [is] controlled by the society or association of self-governing members. These people maintain and improve standards and criteria for entrance and performance in the field of work or occupation."

We may have a lot of people who meet the individual standards of being professionals, but we do not have control by a "society or association of self-governing members." We currently have a window of opportunity for proactively creating such a society or association before serious problems arise that could either damage us during our adolescence as a profession or mobilize us to react by forming the kind of association we need for dealing with matters that can only be handled collectively. White and Wooten propose one proactive alternative—namely, a hierarchical "National Organization Development Association," with national boards for education standards, ethics review, and examination and licensing, and similar boards for each state. Another alternative, which presently exists in nebulous form, is the Human Systems Development Consortium, to which many of the leading OD-oriented professional organizations in the United States have sent representatives in the past. The HSDC might, if it chose to recongregate, create the task forces necessary to enable the profession to set and maintain its education standards, monitor its practice and practitioners (perhaps using peer review or examination and licensing or some combination), and review its ethics. Such an organization would probably look less like a pyramid and more like a wheel, with the central consortium steering committee at the hub, the various member organizations as a ring around the hub, and then the various task forces in an outer ring. In any case, we now have a choice to proact or react, but that choice may not be ours much longer.

For now, the focus is likely to be on national associations, such as the HSDC in the United States, or multinational associations, such as those in Europe, the Western Hemisphere, and Southeast Asia. If we can develop such associations at the national and multinational levels, however, the creation of a global, transnational association, based on the same concentric circle model, seems a reasonable next step.

In thinking about this whole issue of monitoring entry and practice and creating structures to do so, it is important to remember the points raised in discussing the first issue. Of particular importance is keeping our purpose primary and not letting functions and structures get in the way of our ability to serve that purpose.

To What Extent, If Any, is the Profession Responsible for Monitoring the Ethical Practice of its Members?

The above discussion raises one last issue about monitoring practice and practitioners, namely, monitoring the *ethical* practice of our profession's members. The Annotated Statement is a means of providing the kind of educational tool professionals will need to enable themselves to practice ethically. But what happens in case of violations? One option is to wait until they occur and then react. However, many of us would prefer to anticipate possible violations by making our coping methods clear before we need them, thereby reducing the likelihood of violations and preparing ourselves to deal with them effectively in case they do occur. The Statement deals with this issue to some extent in Guideline IV-D:

> Work actively for ethical practice by individuals and organizations engaged in OD-HSD activities and, in case of questionable practice, use appropriate channels for dealing with it.

1. Discuss directly and constructively when feasible.
2. Use other means when necessary, including
   a. Joint consultation and feedback (with another professional as a third party)
   b. Enforcement procedures of existing professional organizations
   c. Public confrontation

Ideally, OD-HSD professionals will behave ethically. If they have questions about one another's ethics, this guideline encourages them to deal with their questions "directly and constructively when feasible." Then, only if necessary, should they use stronger means, turning first to consultation with a third party to try to resolve their differences. In order to achieve uniformity, it is probably desirable to develop professionwide means of preventing violations (such as the Annotated Statement, cases, and issues discussions in Gellermann et al., 1990). We will also need professionwide means of responding to violations when the means of response outlined in guideline IV-D are inadequate. The kind of organization suggested by White and Wooten or an HSDC ethics task force of the kind suggested above are possible channels for response. Again, the question is, Can we mobilize our energy to deal with this need proactively or must we wait until some kind of crisis requires us to deal with it reactively? I would like to believe that the OD-HSD profession can deal with this kind of issue proactively.

In this connection, the caution raised by Kushner (1986, pp. 127-129) in discussing the role of religion is helpful. He says, "A religion which persists in understanding 'good' to mean 'unquestioningly obedient' is a religion which would make perpetual children of us all. . . . Religion should . . . encourage us to challenge its own positions critically not out of adolescent impatience with limits but on the basis of an informed adult conscience." Those ideas apply equally to the role of professions in determining the ethics of their members. In other words, the ultimate responsibility for ethical conduct lies with each professional, and the profession's responsibility is to encourage its members to make their decisions on the basis of "an informed adult conscience."

One final point: It has been observed that "bad tends to drive out good," as for example, bad money driving out good in the case of Gresham's Law of economics. The same can be said about "bad practice driving out good" in the life of a profession. If we do not collectively define what we mean by "good practice" and take collective responsibility for ensuring the prevalence of "good," then it is likely that "bad practice" will prevail. That seems particularly likely for the OD-HSD profession because of the competitive economic conditions within which most of us function. I hasten to add, however, that I believe it is possible to monitor "good practice" in ways that respect the individual responsibility of each of the members of our professional community.

OD-HSD VALUES, RESPONSIBILITIES, AND PRACTICE

Does the Profession Place High Value on "Democratic" Decision Making?

The Statement refers to "appropriate" decision making (Value 3-c), which is a response to criticism of earlier versions that said we valued "democratic" decision making. Most practitioners who responded to the 1983 questionnaire (Gellermann, 1984) accepted the word "democratic," but among them many wanted to recognize explicitly that democratic participation is not practical under all conditions. One person argued against that, however, by saying, "Don't qualify a true statement. Everyone knows that compromise is at times necessary or nothing." Another said, "Placing a high value does not mean a practicing professional will insist on democratic process as the only means in every situation."

Those who support using the word "democratic" are in agreement with Marvin Weisbord, a partner in a leading national consulting firm, who said in a keynote address to a U.S. OD Network conference, "The only thing we bring to the party that other specialists don't is a commitment to democratic processes for achieving desired results."

Comments from those who disagreed included: "The emphasis on democracy as an end is misplaced;" "I don't think we are trying to make all organizations into 'democracies' and this statement creates that image;" "Excludes many OD people;" "Drop democratic decision making. It is not universally relevant to effective problem solving or decision making;" and "I don't like the statement—it commits to an ideology with which I am only sometimes aligned. But I'd rather have it stand than add anything to it."

The view of the people who would like to drop the reference to "democratic decision making" and shift the emphasis to "participation" and "involvement" may be summarized in the words of one respondent, who said, "Equating democratic decision making, which has a strong popular identity as a political process, with involvement and participation, is inaccurate and can create unnecessary resistance among clients. . . . Participation and involvement are sufficiently justified by 'effective problem solving,' improved decision making, and 'organizational excellence'. . . . Our democratic values should be secondary or, better yet, a nonissue."

Is it sufficient to drop the words "democratic decision making" and assume that their meaning is recognized by other words? I concluded that it was not; thus, although the reference to "democratic" decision making was changed, "democracy" was added so that it was explicitly recognized as a value. However, it is important to recognize that it may not be valued by all members of the profession. Part of the apparent aversion to "democracy" by some of us may come from confusing the vision of democracy with the current reality of political process in the United States and elsewhere. Disillusionment with that process can understandably leave people with doubts about democracy. For example, George Bernard Shaw has been quoted as defining democracy as "the substitution of election by the incompetent many for appointment by the corrupt few." However, if we view democracy as government of, by, and for the people, then, in spite of its current limitations, we can choose it as an ideal and work actively to make informed, competent, democratic participation possible, while, at the same time, recognizing its current inadequacies.

Even granting that possibility, however, some people rate other values more highly, such as excellence and efficiency. But many OD-HSD professionals believe it is possible to have excellence and efficiency with democracy and, in the long run, impossible to have them without it. (For evidence that supports the possibility of democracy coexisting with excellence and efficiency, see Mason, 1982; Simmons & Mares, 1983.)

Current reality may limit opportunities for democratic decision making, given the priority of the excellence and efficiency values, but we can still value democracy by encouraging participation and involvement in the present and striving to broaden democracy in the future. A central question is: *Are OD-HSD professionals willing to make democracy a primary value, even when some of their clients seem not to value it?*

To What Extent is the Profession Responsible to Labor Unions, Other Worker Organizations, and Their Representatives?

One respondent to an earlier version of the Statement said, "It's important to recognize the 'cultural differences' between OD-HSD professionals (very individualistic) and many in the labor unions (more communal), [and] for OD-HSD professionals to acknowledge their own tradition and location in the struggle for control of the workplace." He adds, "I assume many . . . involved in this Statement want a more democratic form of business institution. That would seem to lead to a new approach toward the 'union' of workers. . . . Union leaders are looking for new forms of conduct and it seems an appropriate time for us to do so as well."

This is a wide-open issue. OD-HDS practitioners hold widely differing positions: Some are pro-union, others anti-union, and most focus on the ways in which specific unions and their representatives serve (or could serve) the greater good of the organization-system and its stakeholders. Of those concerned about how the union serves the good of the system, some are also concerned with how the system serves the good of the union as one of its primary stakeholders.

The Statement explicitly acknowledges the fact of labor unions and workers' representatives as people whom OD-HSD consultants are expected to inform and involve to the extent appropriate. (See Notes a and b under Guideline III-A-4.) This may create dilemmas in our work with unionized organizations when our employers object to our cooperating with the unions, but it is better to acknowledge such possible dilemmas than to ignore them.

The Statement also, through its expression of general agreement with the United Nations' *Universal Declaration of Human Rights*, implicitly recognizes that "everyone has the right to form and to join trade unions for the protection of his interests" (Article 23, Point 4 of the declaration per Williams, 1981).

At the present time, it seems inappropriate for the Statement to refer to the responsibilities of OD-HSD consultants to labor unions and workers' representatives any more explicitly than it currently does. These groups are clearly stakeholders in many of our client systems, and as such are due the same consideration given to other stakeholders, including managers. Because we are frequently employed by managers in business systems, such a stance may seem wrong or at least controversial. However, if we accept the whole system as our client and commit ourselves to serving the interests of all its stakeholders, we have a responsibility to them. This does not deny the practical and ethical dilemmas mentioned earlier in discussing the questions "Who is our client?" and "To whom are we responsible and for what?"

To What Extent, If Any, Do We Recognize Responsibility for Helping Organizations and Other Human Systems Provide for the Fair and Just Distribution of the Fruits of Their Productivity Among All of Their Stakeholders?

As an example of this issue, consider a situation in which an OD-HSD professional facilitates an employee participation program that results in a substantial increase in productivity. Does she have an ethical responsibility for encouraging the fair and just distribution of that increase? Some people would not even consider the question. Others would say no. Still others would say that the employees who contributed to the increase should get some part of it, but opinions vary widely about how much they should receive and about the role of OD-HSD professionals in implementing the distribution.

The exact nature of this issue is still vaguely defined, since it can extend beyond concerns about sharing productivity increases to the question of how to establish equity in salaries, wages, and compensation generally. There are many organizations in which managers as well as workers feel they are not fairly treated by the existing compensation system, but feel powerless to change it. They talk as if they still want to contribute to the best of their ability, but their motivation must inevitably be affected negatively and with substantial loss in productivity, creativity, and satisfaction as a result.

This issue also extends beyond compensation to the question of how to establish fairness and equity for customers, stockholders, suppliers, governments, communities, and all of a system's stakeholders in sharing the fruits of its productivity. Equitable sharing is an ethical issue of primary importance for the OD-HSD profession; the Statement recognizes the promotion of justice as one of the profession's social responsibilities (Guideline V-C). However, as noted in the discussion under Guideline V-C-1, our role is more one of facilitating decisions about equity than of prescribing what is equitable.

For OD-HSD Professionals Who Work with Business Organizations, How is Profitability to be Valued Relative to Other Values?

In an article about corporate moral development, Johnson & Johnson has been identified as one of the best examples of an ethical corporation (Reidenbach & Robin, 1989). Its credo shows a strong balance between concern for profits and concern for the interests of all stakeholders. That credo articulates the company's responsibilities in the following sequence: first, to its consumers ("doctors, nurses, patients, and mothers who buy our products and services"); second, to its employees; third, to all the communities with which it deals, "including the community of man"; and finally, to its stockholders. After listing these various groups in that order, the credo continues to say: "We have often been asked why we put the stockholder last . . . and our answer has always been that, if we do the other jobs properly . . . the stockholder will always be well served. The record suggests that this is the case." As part of the record, Johnson & Johnson's experience with the Tylenol crisis—in which some of its product was tampered with, resulting in massive, expensive recalls—illustrates how the credo was so much a part of the firm's way of life that its senior managers did not hesitate to recall regardless of cost.

Another perspective on the relative value to be given to profit is offered by Russell Ackoff (1986) when he talks about profit as necessary for the survival of a business enterprise, but not the reason for it. As he says, profit is a requirement, not an objective; a means, not an end. He then expresses his conviction that those who manage corporations do so primarily to provide themselves with a quality of work life and standard of living that are good for them, rather than to maximize profit and growth. And, rather than apologizing for that objective, he contends that it should be extended to cover the quality of working life and living standard of all employees. He then puts quality of life and standard of living into perspective by emphasizing that they cannot be improved without making a profit, paying dividends large enough to attract and retain investors, increasing productivity, and providing for growth.

In combination, the Johnson & Johnson and Ackoff perspectives—the first with its focus on the degree of responsibility to some of the most important stakeholders in business, and the second with its focus on quality of work life and standard of living as primary values of senior managers and on profit as a means rather than an end—suggest ways of thinking about profit that may make decisions by OD-HSD professionals easier. These perspectives involve reframing our concept of "the bottom line" (profit) as primary, and seeing it as a means to serving other values, particularly the quality of life and standard of living values of senior managers, customers, employees, and communities. Within that new framework, it is much easier to think practically about how to serve those values as well as the other values we consider most important.

In the last analysis, however, our most difficult ethical choices will come down to acting in ways that are good and right because they are good and right, and not because they can be rationalized as being in the narrowly defined self-interest of the people with whom we contract. As the Statement notes, when we cannot act in ways that we consider ethical, we should withhold or withdraw our services (Guidelines II-A and V-D).

The importance of profitability is implicitly recognized in the Annotated Statement (annotation following the Preamble) with the following words: "Among other things, we seek to facilitate the development of human systems as healthy settings within which individuals can grow *in ways that enable those systems to survive and thrive economically so they can continue to be healthy settings*" (emphasis added).

Is it Appropriate to Found Our Value System on "Happiness"?

The introductory note in the Values section of the Annotated Statement says that "Our value system is based on: (1) life and the quest for happiness, (2) freedom, responsibility, and self-control, and (3) justice. When we give these values primary importance and then build on that foundation, these values have the priority that is implicit in our vision of 'people living meaningful, productive, good lives.' " In the discussion of that value, we identify happiness as meaning "whole lives well lived" in contrast to "the momentary satisfaction associated with satisfying momentary desires." And later, in the discussion of fundamental human rights, we quote Adler (1987, p. 59) as saying that "*the primary right is the pursuit of happiness, having its foundation in our moral obligation to make good lives for ourselves*" (emphasis added). We then call attention to the fact that the right is not to happiness, but rather to the *pursuit* of (or quest for) happiness—namely, people's opportunities-obligations to "make good lives."

Although we acknowledge that happiness is not a right, I contend that we value it above all other values. However, in my experience, we seldom, if ever, talk about it in our role as OD-HSD professionals. I think this is attributable, at least in part, to our work with profit-making organizations in which happiness tends to be regarded irrelevant to, if not bad for, profits. As noted in the earlier discussion, profitability and happiness are not necessarily opposing values, although they may clash in specific short-term situations. In the long run, many of us believe both values are essential to the success of human systems, particularly businesses that function within a free labor market.

In order to make the case more completely for happiness as a primary value, we need to reflect on what we mean by it. Adler's ideas (1987) are helpful. He points out that "happiness is not only an ultimate good to be sought for its own sake, and never as a means to anything beyond itself. It is also the one complete good. . . . When happiness is achieved, it leaves nothing more to be desired, for it involves the possession of all other goods" (p. 52).

Adler then looks closely at two different, though related, concepts of happiness. "One is the modern psychological conception of happiness as a feeling of contentment produced by the satisfaction we experience when we are able to fulfill whatever desires we happen to have at any moment in time. The other is the ancient ethical conception of happiness as a whole life well lived because it is enriched by the cumulative possession of all the goods that a morally virtuous human being ought to desire" (p. 52).

As noted earlier, it is the "whole life will lived" concept of happiness that we consider primary. Having said that, it will help to clarify what we mean by "well lived" in that concept. Again Adler (1987, pp. 54–55) is helpful by his differentiation between two kinds of desires. "One set of desires consists of wants human beings acquire in the course of their individual lives. . . . Such desires differ from person to person. . . . Another set of desires consists of the needs that all human beings share in common . . . [which] we normally speak of . . . as our natural needs." Then he describes how our desires can guide our lives by noting that "our needs are always right desires, desires for the real goods we ought to desire, whereas our wants may be either right or wrong desires." Adler illustrates how a "want" can be a "wrong desire" by referring to "individuals who want power or domination over others and are willing to infringe on the freedom of others in order to satisfy their desires" (p.

55). [Note: This relates to our ethical principles about not acting in ways that "treat people only as means" and that "increase the power of more powerful stakeholders *over* the less powerful"; also to the discussion that suggests an ethical alternative that can increase the power available to managers by focusing on empowerment and power *with*.]

Based on these ideas, Adler asserts that a life "well lived" is guided by the prescription that "we *ought* to seek everything that is *really* good for us and . . . there is nothing else we *ought* to seek . . . Since happiness, ethically conceived, is the complete good of a whole life enriched by the cumulative possession of everything *really* good for us, the self-evident prescription just stated is equivalent to saying that we *ought* to seek happiness, that we are morally obliged to pursue it" (p. 57). For those of us who accept that idea, we believe that OD-HSD professionals "ought" to value happiness in the ethical sense of "a whole life well lived" and, therefore, believe that our profession's ethics "ought" to guide our behavior and our efforts to influence others' behavior in accordance with that value. We recognize that "ought" and "really good" are not always clear concepts in specific situations, but we accept responsibility for doing the best we can to act consistently with them. We do so not out of blind obedience to the tyranny of should or ought, but because we value happiness.

In the last analysis, we know we are living in accordance with that value, rather than just talking about it, when we meet the test for self-respect described by Nathaniel Branden in an audio recording (1985): "It has to do with knowing in the wee hours of the morning that: knowing the good, we have done it; seeing the beautiful, we have served it; knowing the truth, we have spoken it."

In short, our own happiness is in large part a function of the degree to which we are able to serve others' happiness as well as our own. And our ability to do that is in turn a function of our possession of moral virtue, defined by Adler (1987, p. 54) as "the settled habit or disposition of will to desire what we ought to desire." The discussion of values in the Statement is intended to help us do that.

When OD-HSD professionals talk about "quality of life" as a value, they are focusing on essentially the same thing as happiness. It contrasts with mechanistic values that ignore the quality of people's lives and treat people as objects to be used only in the service of system purposes without regard for their personal purposes. One manifestation of this value is the QWL effort by a number of organizations. It should be recognized, however, that when we refer to "quality of life" we mean all of people's lives and not only the parts they devote to work. We also mean *whole* life (from birth to death) and *all* life (not just the lives of our clients and their immediate stakeholders).

In order to understand more fully the happiness value, we also need to examine more closely two related values that focus on individual human beings.

- *Individuals are valued as whole persons, not only as employees or as means for achieving organizational results.* Tannenbaum and Davis (1969, p. 7) wrote of this when they referred to movement away from avoidance or negative evaluation of individuals and toward confirming them as human beings. Among other things, it means caring about them personally, including their concerns, hopes, desires, and fears, as well as their productive strengths and weaknesses. By recognizing the *whole* person, OD-HSD practice seeks to empower people to express their full potential in their jobs and their lives generally. For example, this is reflected when an organization supports a person's development even when it may mean the person's eventually leaving the organization.
- *Personal growth is valued as well as the growth of job-related competence.* Organizations may question whether it is their responsibility to encourage growth that does not directly serve their purposes, but OD-HSD practice tends to assume that without attending to people's full growth potential, the portion that is organizationally relevant is likely to suffer. There may even be a widely shared judgment that ignoring or hindering personal growth simply because it does not serve organizational purposes is morally wrong.

The place of happiness in the relationship between human systems and human beings may be described in the following parable:

> A sinner is being shown heaven and hell. He sees two large doors and is led through one of them, which he assumes at first is the door to heaven because of the wonderful aroma of delectable foods that greets him. As he enters he sees a number of people sitting around a large round table. He notices that despite the wonderful feast in the middle, the people look emaciated and groan with hunger. Each has a spoon with a very long handle that can reach the food in the middle. But because the handles are so much longer than their arms, none can get the food into their mouths. They suffer terribly from the unceasing hunger and frustration, and the man realizes he is in hell. He is then led through the other door to see heaven. At first he sees what looks

like the same situation—the same delicious food, the same large table, people sitting around it with long-handled spoons. But these people look cheerful and well fed, and they are chatting and laughing. The man is puzzled and asks what the difference is here. The reply: They have learned to feed each other. (quoted in Wachtel, 1989, pp. 189–190)

Using the imagery of the parable, we could say that if human systems and human beings could learn to feed each other, we might change life on earth from hell for many to heaven for all. And the OD-HSD profession, if we choose to do so, can play an important role in achieving that transformation.

Does Ethics Clarification Have a Place Among the Services Offered by OD-HSD Professionals?

In the personal, group, organizational, and system development that the OD-HSD profession has offered historically, helping people clarify their ethics and develop their ability to act in accord with consciously chosen ethical standards has not been central to the practitioner's role. However, the need for such service has become increasingly clear recently, particularly in the United States, where ethical problems in business and government have received a great deal of attention during the late 1980s and early 1990s. Jerry Harvey, a leader in the profession since its inception, was recently quoted as saying that "the only emerging role that is available" for OD consultants is one that "focuses on the moral, ethical, and spiritual aspects of work" (Chase, 1989, p. 8).

Business in particular could benefit from the attention of OD-HSD professionals because collectively we have an interest in the functioning of both the whole business system and our individual client systems-organizations as well. By acting assertively to support the ethical leadership of industrial associations and professions related to business—such as the various science, engineering, and management professional associations and societies—the OD-HSD profession could enhance the forces that encourage individual business organizations to behave in ways that are good for their industries and society as well as their own interests. Given competitive market conditions, people who work for individual enterprises are under great pressure to behave in ways that serve the narrowly defined interests of their enterprises. Ethical leadership by industrial and professional associations can serve as a countervailing force to that of competition when it works against the good of society. And the OD-HSD profession-as-a-whole, in contrast to its individual members, is uniquely qualified to encourage such leadership.

To What Extent, If Any, Do We Recognize "Love" as a Dimension in the Practice of OD-HSD?

The Annotated Statement refers to "love" when it says that "the OD-HSD profession aspires to help people realize their highest potential, individually and collectively, by . . . supporting the creation and maintenance of a climate within which freedom, mutual trust, respect, and love prevail" (Belief 4-f). Those words are adapted from a policy statement developed by senior executives at Kollmorgen, a medium-sized electronics company (Kiefer & Stroh, 1983, p. 27). Many people in our field explicitly or implicitly refer to love as in Tannenbaum's question, "Does this path have a heart?" However, as the Annotated Statement notes in its discussion of that belief, the reference to love is controversial, with some practitioners wanting to delete the word because it is "not necessary for organizational functioning," and others contending, "That's what OD is all about."

Given the systems perspective of our work, it is helpful to note Albert Einstein's view:

> A human being is part of a whole, called by us the 'universe,' a part limited in time and space. He experiences himself, his thought and feelings as some thing separated from the rest—a kind of optical delusion of his consciousness. This delusion is a kind of prison for us, restricting us to our personal desires and to affection for a few persons nearest to us. Our task must be to free ourselves from this prison by widening our circle of compassion to embrace all living creatures and the whole of nature in its beauty. Nobody is able to achieve this completely, but the striving for such achievement is in itself a part of the liberation and a foundation for inner security. (Quoted in Pedrazzini & Gable, 1989, p. 3)

Answering the question, Does love have a place in our practice? requires us to ask ourselves further questions: What *do* we stand for? If love *is* important to us, what do we mean by it? These questions are not easily answered. In specifying what we mean by *love*, we can say that, among other things, we mean compassion (as in the Einstein quotation) and caring. In elaborating on these concepts, we will need to deal with the apparent contradiction between conditional and unconditional love, sometimes differentiated as the love of the father and mother. In commenting on how we can deal with that contradiction, one respondent to the Statement said, "It involves a dialectic between reason and feelings; a thesis, antithesis, and synthesis in which reason and feelings nourish each other." It is also helpful to note that such a dialectic will need to recognize differences in reasoning processes between males and females of the kind identified by Carol Gilligan, who discovered that "boys tend to apply abstract concepts like rights and justice to dilemmas, while girls [think] more about relationships" (Brown, 1987, p. 3). Love is clearly in the concrete realm of relationships and, though we do not have sufficient basis for generalizing, it is interesting to note that it has been men who have most strongly objected to acknowledging that love has a place in our practice, although many men have been equally as strong in support of its inclusion.

Our purpose at this point is not to resolve the issue, but only to identify it. For some of us, the answer is clear that love not only has a place in our practice, but is, in fact, at the heart of it. However, we also recognize that we still have much to do in clarifying what we mean by that.

To What Extent, If Any, Is "Beauty" Among the Most Important of Our OD-HSD Values?

This issue is at the horizon of our frontier issues. Its nature is suggested by Pedrazzini and Gable (1989, p. 16):

It has been suggested that aesthetics will be the ethics of the future. This idea makes a great deal of sense in a world of rapid change with the need for continual adaptation and evolution. This concept would make integrity, which is a biologically, and socially sound concept, the basis for ethics. Management is finding that those people who are congruent in their 'thinking, behaving, and believing' are the most successful in leading their organizations through change. There is a power in having integrated responses to situations [that] people can rely on. Responsibility flows from integrity. When human systems are integrated, they become able to respond as needed to achieve desired goals . . . The aesthetic perspective includes a world of 'other means' for which there is no verbal referent. The experience, like the image, is prior to the word and contains more knowledge. This perspective makes a unity of reason and intuition and provides the grounding for 'common sensing' and consensus.

To make the link between esthetics and beauty explicit we need also to include the dictionary definition of *esthetic*: namely, "related to the beautiful as distinguished from the merely pleasing, moral, and [especially] the useful and utilitarian . . . [and] appreciative of, responsive to, or zealous about the beautiful" (Pedrazzini & Gable, 1989, p. 16).

FIGURE 3.1   LIVING WITH VISION.

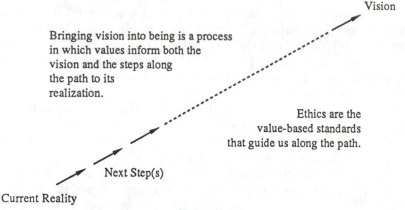

Source: Adapted from Kiefer and Stroh, 1983.

From another perspective, the relationship of ethics to beauty may be described using a metaphor. A model for thinking about vision, current reality, and the process of bringing vision into being is described in Figure 3.1.

In the model, vision refers to an "image" in the mind's eye (including feelings as well as visual images) of a desired state. For an individual, it could be reflected in a person's answer to the question, What would your life be like if it were exactly the way you would like it to be? For organization members it could reflect their answer to the question, What would your organization be like if it were exactly the way you would like it to be? For example, at the individual level, Alexander Graham Bell was guided by a vision of the communication device we now call "the telephone." And, at the organizational level, in 1908, before we had satellites and transoceanic cables, a vision for the American Telephone and Telegraph Company was conceived as "a communication system that would enable anyone anywhere to communicate with anyone anywhere anytime." There may have been other dimensions to that vision, but that example illustrates how words can reflect a vision even when the technology for bringing the vision into being does not exist and when many people may believe that such a vision is impossible.

In thinking about vision, it is important to note that it reflects the esthetic perspective that Pedrazzini and Gable (1989) described as being one that exists "prior to the word" and, therefore, "contains more knowledge." In this connection, note also the relevance of the idea that "a picture is worth a thousand words."

According to the model in Figure 3.1, one need not know about how one is going to realize one's vision, but only to be clear about (a) one's "vision" (although it may change and become richer and more complex over time), (b) "current reality" (namely, that which is currently going on within and around one's self or one's organization or whatever social entity is involved in visioning); and (c) one's "next steps." With regard to "next steps," the meaning of that idea is well conveyed by Confucius's expression that "a journey of ten thousand miles starts with but a single step." One need not have a comprehensive plan for achieving one's vision, only a willingness to take each next step one at a time.

The place of values and ethics in the process of living with vision is also noted in the model: (a) values which are standards of *importance*, inform both the vision and the step-by-step process of realization, and (b) ethics, which are value-based standards of *behavior*, provide guidance for taking each step.

This discussion began by saying that a metaphor could be used to describe the relationship of ethics to beauty. If the life paths of individuals, from current reality to the realization of their visions, are conceived of as multicolored threads, then to the extent that those threads come together in the creation of the lives of organizations and other human systems, they can be conceived collectively as a tapestry. And, if that tapestry is esthetically satisfying, we can say that those lives are "beautiful" (as well as being "meaningful, productive, and good" in accordance with the vision described in the Statement). In that context, values and ethics have a fundamental place in determining the beauty of the tapestry; or, perhaps, beauty lies behind those values and ethics that "should" guide us in our "quest for a good life."

From another perspective, the metaphor is useful in thinking about our role as OD-HSD professionals and as a profession. If we conceive of human beings as the weavers of their own lives, we can conceive of ourselves as meta-weavers who help people learn to weave together in a way that creates a beautiful whole.

To What Extent, If Any, Do We Recognize "Spirit" as a Dimension in the Practice of OD-HSD?

Responses to the May 1983 Statement suggested including the following as one of the assumptions underlying the guidelines: "Human beings are . . . interdependent economically, politically, socially, culturally, and spiritually and are responsible for the choices they make within that context" (Belief 1-c). The spiritual reference was added because one person identified "starting a spiritual incre-ment" as one of the central purposes of the profession and another person specifically suggested including *spiritual* in the words quoted above. In contrast, two people asked, "Is this a profession or a religion?"

Just as some people's experience with democratic political process can leave them with an aversion to democracy, the experience of others with established religions can leave them with an aversion to religion. Regardless of how practitioners feel about "religion," they may still be able to acknowledge that "spirit" is a dimension in the practice of OD-HSD, even if only in the sense of "team spirit."

As an example of how the issue of spiritual consciousness is becoming more visible, two highly experienced practitioners, Billie Alban and Sheldon Hughes, in a presentation to the New York OD Network (Diagonali, 1984), talked about their discovery "that managers are indeed looking for a deeper spiritual base upon which to build." They invited OD professionals "to be inspired, emboldened, and encouraged to infuse our training and consulting practices with our hearts, minds, and spirits." Even more significantly, an indicator of what is going on at this frontier is the transformational movement that treats "spirit" as primary. (For example, see Owen, 1987.)

The key questions underlying this issue are: Do we acknowledge spirit as an aspect of reality with which OD-HSD practice must deal? And, if so, how do we deal with it? As a first step toward answering these questions, Ken Wilbur's ideas are clarifying. Wilbur (1983, p. 70) says that we need to recognize that mind can adequately look at and map sense data because it transcends them; it can adequately look at and map intellectual data because they are its own creation; "but it cannot adequately look at and map spirit because spirit transcends it." The challenge for us as a profession is to find or create ways of gathering data about the realm of the spirit in ways that can be independently replicated by others and then interpreted in ways that allow for consensual validation, thereby enabling ourselves to move ahead together in serving our common purpose as fully as we are able.[5]

One final point also needs to be made. The possibility that spirit may be at the core of our ability to act morally and ethically is suggested by Ralph Waldo Emerson (1988, p. 8):

---

[5] The practice of meditation, as described by Herbert Benson, M.D., associate professor of medicine at the Harvard Medical School, in his book, *The Relaxation Response* (1976), has the potential of being one such way.

The lessons of the moral sentiment are, once for all, an emancipation from that anxiety which takes the joy out of all life. . . . It is a commandment at every moment and in every condition of life to do the duty of that moment and to abstain from doing the wrong. And it is so near and inward and constitutional to each, that no commandment can compare with it in authority. All wise men regard it as the voice of the Creator himself.

Harman and Rheingold (1984, pp. 109–110) express a similar idea in terms of its relation to our contemporary times:

The last great transformation of public beliefs regarding the proper source of values and guidance occurred nearly a thousand year ago, when the other-worldly perspective of the Middle Ages changed to the pragmatic, secular earth-oriented world-view that produced the Renaissance, the Industrial Revolution and the world we live in today. . . . In the midst of the ruin of our former value systems, an old message is surfacing, stated in modern terms: *Guidance can be found, and the authority is the most trustworthy possible mentor— one's own higher self.*

CONCLUSION

Building on the foundation of the generally agreed-upon values described in the Annotated Statement and the additional values suggested in this discussion, the OD-HSD profession appears now to be in a position to resolve constructively the issues that have been discussed, as well as others that will emerge as the field continues to evolve in its collective consciousness of what it is. Even more importantly, the profession can be expected to continue defining and refining its mission in the world and, as a result, gain a heightened sense of itself as a global professional community. That mission seems likely to involve helping people achieve and maintain excellence as individuals, as organizations, and as other human systems—at levels far above most people's present levels of aspiration. Some people would even say that the highest level involves realizing, both in the sense of "becoming aware" and "bringing into being," the essential divinity that they believe exists within all human beings. Primary among the conditions that will make that highest achievement possible is the uniting of OD-HSD professionals throughout the world in a community committed to the realization of a common vision—namely, a vision that can be expressed as "people living meaningful, productive, good lives in ways that simultaneously serve them, their organizations, their societies, and the world" (from the Preamble of the Statement).

ADDENDA

In reflecting on the preceding discussion, there are two points I would particularly like to add.

The function of profit in business value systems is becoming clearer and OD-HSD professionals have an important role to play in helping business people clarify that function. The preceding discussion raised the question "How is profitibility to be valued relative to other values [of business organizations]?" In responding to that question, the importance of valuing the interests of *all* stakeholders, rather than making stockholders primary, and viewing profit as a means to serving business purposes, rather than as the reason for business existence, were discussed. The function of profit deserves further consideration.

One view of business is that its *only* social responsibility is maximizing return to shareholders. The value base for that standard is "profit maximization" and the standard that value can produce is "act in any way that contributes to maximizing return." The result over time has been recurring behavior that by societal standards is generally considered unethical or even immoral, not to mention illegal. Examples include: (a) the Morton-Thiokol engineers and managers who approved the space shuttle Challenger's lift-off in spite of the fact that they knew the booster rocket's O-rings would not function properly at temperatures below freezing; (b) the people within the asbestos industry who, years ago, suppressed publication of information about the connection between cancer and breathing asbestos fibers; (c) defense contractors who delivered products to the military that had not been tested according to the specifications of their contracts; and (d) executives in an automobile company who consciously chose not to correct life-threatening defects in their cars because the expected costs to the business of death and injury would be less than the cost of correcting the defects.

Making profit the *primary* value of a business tends to create what Laura Nash (1990) calls "bottom-line blindness." As she explains

> When profit becomes the dominant purpose it is not just prioritized, it is "exclusified." Profit is so concrete and "strong" a claim and ethics so abstract and process-oriented that the former can easily gain dominion over one's decision making.

Corporations have already begun to overcome bottom-line blindness as a result of adding "total quality" and "service orientation" to the equation that defines what business is all about. Also, according to a study by the American Management Association, "integrity" was identified as the managerial quality most admired by managers. We may well be moving toward corporate cultures that balance profit as a primary value with quality, service, and integrity—and, perhaps, other values as well. OD-HSD professionals, individually and collectively, are uniquely qualified to facilitate such fundamental changes in the culture of business.

In this connection, it is helpful to note that in thinking about how to communicate with managers about the narrowness of the profit-maximizing, self-interest-oriented model of business ethics, Nash (1990) provides an excellent critique. As an alternative, she develops a model based on *creating delivered value* and *mutual benefit* (including profit). Her views have been well received by CEOs of NYNEX, Champion International, Hill and Knowlton, and a former CEO of Ford Motor Company.

The "self-fulfilling prophecy" is important to the way in which we choose to conceive of ourselves as a profession and the purpose, vision, and values we share as members of that profession. The point made at the beginning of this discussion—namely that a potential advance in our communal self-concept is of "ourselves as a community capable of facilitating the emergence of a global community whose life is coordinated by shared consciousness of a common purpose, vision, values, and ethics"—deserves special emphasis against the background of the discussion. That advance would be consistent with our purpose and vision, as articulated in the Statement—particularly our vision's emphasis on "people living meaningful, productive, good lives in ways that simultaneously serve them, their organizations, their societies, and the world"— and it seems a logical extension of our coordinating our practice in relation to bringing that vision into being. Furthermore, it is consistent with our core values, as articulated in the Statement— including love of life, quest for happiness (whole lives well lived), freedom, responsibility, self-control, and justice.

Some may say that such an aspiration is too grandiose. On the other hand, it helps to remember the concept of the self-fulfilling prophecy, namely a belief which, when acted upon, tends to bring the belief into being. For example, the Great Depression in the United States during the 1930s is said to have been the result of such a widely shared belief. If the community of OD-HSD professionals is going to make a mistake, either on the side of caution or on the side of dreaming great dreams, I would prefer to err on the side of great dreams so that we will have the self-fulfilling prophecy effect working for us rather than against us.[6]

REFERENCES

Ackoff, R. (1986), *Management in small doses*. New York: John Wiley & Sons.

Adler, M. (1987). *We hold these truths: Understanding the ideas and ideals of the constitution*. New York: Macmillan.

Benson, H., M.D. (with M. Klipper). (1976). *The relaxation response*. New York: Avon.

Branden, N. (1985). Building self-esteem [Audiocassette]. Washington, DC: American Psychological Association.

Brown, M. (1987). Care and justice. *Organizational Ethics Newsletter, 4* (9), 3–5.

Chase, T. (1989, October). Monthly quote. *New York Organization Development Network Newsletter* p. 8.

Diagonali, J. (1984, February). December NYODN meeting. *New York Organization Development Network Newsletter*, pp. 2–4.

Emerson, R. (1988, February). Monthly quote. *New York Organization Development Newsletter*, February, p. 8.

Gellermann, W. (1984). Issues in developing a statement of values and ethics for organization development professionals. *Organization Development Journal, 2* (1), 39–47.

Gellermann, W. (1985). Values and ethical issues for human systems development. In R. Tannenbaum, N. Margulies & F. Massarik and Associates, *Human systems development* (pp. 393–418). San Francisco: Jossey-Bass.

Gellermann, W. (1990, September). The core of professional identity: Common purpose, values, and ethics. *OD Practitioner, 22* (3), 1–3.

Gellermann, W., Frankel, M., & Ladenson, R. (1990). *Values and ethics in organization and human systems development: Responding to dilemmas in professional life*. San Francisco, CA: Jossey-Bass.

---

[6] To make the possibility of OD's "facilitating the emergence of a global community" more real, it may help to cite some examples of how this might be done. These include such activities as: support for creation of a global vision (as described above); the work done by a team of OD professionals in facilitating a "Conference On A More Democratic United Nations," which discussed, among other things, the creation of a Second People's Assembly whose members would represent "the people," in contrast to the representation of national governments given by the General Assembly; and the creation of a European East-West Organization Development Network to facilitate the European integration process (organized by a group of professionals at conferences in Bulgaria during 1990 and 1991).

Goodstein, L., & Hunt, J. (1981). Commentary: Do American theories apply abroad. *Organizational Dynamics, 10* (1), 49–62.

Harman, W., Ph.D., & Rheingold, H., (1984). *Higher creativity: Liberating the unconscious for breakthrough insights.* Los Angeles, CA: Jeremy P. Tarcher.

Hinckley, S., Jr. (1986, October). *Challenges facing the profession of human systems development.* Paper presented at Certified Consultants International conference, New York.

Hofstede, G. (1980). "Motivation, leadership and organization: Do American theories apply abroad?" *Organizational Dynamics, 9* (1), 42–68.

Hofstede, G. (1981). Do American theories apply abroad: A reply to Goodstein and Hunt. *Organizational Dynamics, 10* (1), 63–68.

Kiefer, C., & Stroh, P. (1983). A new paradigm for organization development. *Training and Development Journal, 37,* (4), 26–35.

Kushner, H. (1986). *When all you ever wanted isn't enough: The search for a life that matters.* New York: Pocket Books.

Mason, R. (1982). *Participatory and workplace democracy.* Carbondale, IL: Southern Illinois University.

Nash, L. (1990), *Good intentions aside: A manager's guide to solving ethical problems.* Boston, MA: Harvard Business School Press.

Owen, H. (1987). *Spirit: Transformation and development in organizations.* Potomac, MD: Abbott Publishing.

Pedrazzini, L., & Gable, C, (1989, November). *Art as a tool for self-integration in the workplace.* Unpublished paper presented at the Organizational Development Network National Conference, San Diego, CA.

Reidenbach, R. E., & Robin, D. (1989). *A conceptual model of corporate moral development.* Unpublished paper presented at the 1989 Conference of the Society for Business Ethics.

Russell, P. (1983). *The global brain: Speculations on the evolutionary leap to planetary consciousness.* Los Angeles: J.P. Tarcher, Inc.

Shepard, H. (1983, Summer). The irony of a mature helping profession. *CCI News,* pp. 6–7.

Simmons, J., & Mares, W. (1983). *Working together.* New York: Knopf.

Tannenbaum, R., & Davis, S. (1969). Values, man and organizations. In W. Eddy & others (Eds.), *Behavioral science and the manager's role.* Washington, DC: NTL Institute for Applied Behavioral Science.

Wachtel, P. (1989). *The poverty of affluence.* Philadelphia: New Society Publishers.

White, L., & Wooten, K. (1986). *Professional ethics and practice in organizational development.* New York: Praeger.

Wilbur, K. (1983). *Eye to eye: The quest for the new paradigm.* Garden City, NY: Anchor Books.

Williams, P. (Ed. 1981). *The international bill of human rights.* Glen Ellen, CA: Entwhistle Books.

4

Beyond Lewin's Force Field: A New Model for Organizational Change Interventions

Jeffrey Goldstein
Department of Administrative Sciences
Schools of Business
Adelphi University

INTRODUCTION

Organizational change efforts have been deeply influenced by Lewin's "force field" analysis utilized to identify factors either encouraging or resisting change. The "force field" analysis sets the stage, in turn, for using another OD approach derived from Lewin: his threefold change strategy of "unfreezing" the resistance, moving the organization, and "refreezing" the new state. Underlying these Lewinian methods, however, are assumptions about systemic change which have been seriously challenged by recent research into nonlinear, nonequilibrium, and "chaotic" systems. As a result, OD practices derived from Lewin's work need to be reevaluated and alternatives founded on the new research can now be proposed.

To accomplish this reevaluation, first, Lewin's approach and its associated OD methods will be reviewed. Next, basic principles about systemic change emerging from the new research will be outlined. Finally, OD perspectives and practices suggested by the new research will be described.

LEWIN'S MODEL: EQUILIBRIUM AND LINEAR ASSUMPTIONS

Equilibrium-Seeking Social Systems

Like other social-science theories which borrowed the concept of equilibrium from physics (Russet, 1966), Lewin's (1951) "force-field" analysis conceived social systems as an equilibrium of op-

FIGURE 4.1. LEWIN'S FORCE-FIELD ANALYSIS

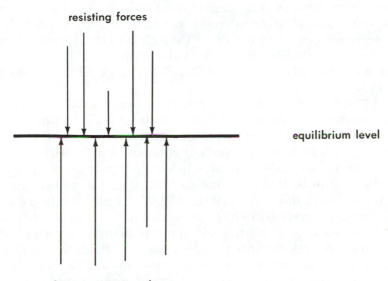

posing forces balanced at "quasi-stationary equilibrium levels" (see Figure 4.1). By equalizing tensions throughout the system, the equilibrium of forces maintains system stability. Lewin defined the equilibrium level by the equation (1951, p. 204):

Fc(forces toward change) + Fr(forces resisting change) = 0

An increase of force on one side increases tension in the system, leading to one of two possible outcomes: (a) a corresponding increase in the opposing force, or (b) a shift in the system to a new equilibrium level in the direction of the increased force. In either case, the equilibrium equation will again equal zero and the system will regain stability.

For example, the "force field" of a factory work group may be balanced at an equilibrium level designating a specific level of productivity. Forces tending toward a higher output might be expertise of the workers, management emphasis on productivity, and good working conditions. Forces resisting this change may be hourly pay, union work rules, and low morale. As long as these forces are in balance, equilibrium-seeking dynamics will keep the work group producing at the specific output equivalent to the equilibrium level.

However, adding a piece-rate pay system could increase the force on the side tending to higher productivity. Tension in the system is thereby increased resulting in either: (a) an increase in an opposing force such as an increase in union resistance based on a claim that the piece-rate formula is unfair, or (b) a shift in the system to a new equilibrium level of higher productivity output. In the latter case, change in the social system is a shift from one equilibrium level to another.

The "force-field" diagram (Figure 4.1) suggests that change is a simple matter of *linearly* (more on linearity shortly) adding force to the progressive side of the balance. But Lewin realized that something else was going on that further resisted change: "Historic constancy creates an 'additional force field' which tends to keep up the present level in addition to whatever other forces are keeping the social process at that level" (1951, p. 225). These "additional force fields" consist of vested interests, institutionalizations of policy, and social habits. All three of these social mechanisms reinforce systemic equilibrium-seeking since they increase resistance to change as a compensation for increases in progressive forces. When a change is introduced into the organization or work group, the "additional force fields" help keep the resultant of the opposing forces at zero. Hence, for Lewin, social systems in their core are resistant to change.

The challenge, then, is how to expedite change in the face of these resistant "additional force fields." Here, Lewin introduced the idea of "unfreezing" the "additional force fields" by means of some kind of catharsis, emotional stirring-up, or group participation (1951, p. 230). Since, by definition, the "additional force field" is an *inherent* part of the organization's functioning, it must be "unfrozen" by some *externally* applied orchestration of activities. The group itself cannot be responsible for quickening the proposed change since it is so highly enmeshed in the "additional force fields." Accordingly, the change agent(s) (whether external or internal) must be perspicacious enough to identify the specific "additional force fields" and clever enough to design appropriate "unfreezing" strategies. Therefore, the emphasis is on extensive *planning* as the key to successful change interventions—hence, the term "planned change" as a synonym for OD. It is this extensive planning that hopefully enables the change agent(s) to get the organization moving. The consequence of taking on such a large burden of responsibility for the change is either glory or frustration for the change agent(s).

After the social system is "unfrozen" and shifted to a new equilibrium level, this new level must be buttressed by "refreezing". An example of the latter would be a new reward system for a desired change in behavior (Burke, 1987, p. 58). The "refreezing" is necessary because the "additional force field" is still liable to pull the group back to its previous equilibrium level. The change agent must anticipate and prevent this backsliding by sufficiently bracing the new level. Similar to the case of "unfreezing", the group itself has little responsibility for maintaining its changed status. Instead, auxiliary and external systems plus the change agent(s) share the responsibility of preserving the changed condition. Again, there is a focus on comprehensive planning as the determining factor for whether the change effort "sticks".

Linearity in Lewin's Change Strategy

Complementing the equilibrium-seeking foundation of Lewin's approach is the equally important assumption of linearity. Since the ramifications of this linearity are important with respect to the OD practices derived from Lewin's model, the mathematical basis of linearity needs to be spelled out in some detail. "Linear" is being used in contrast to nonlinear equations (West, 1985). Thus, a linear equation of the form: $y = ax + b$ (where "y" and "x" are two related variables, and "a" and "b" are constants) implies that the relation between the two variables can be depicted as a straight *line* on a graph. Lewin's "quasi-stationary equilibrium level" equation [$Fc + Fr = 0$] is linear because it can be expressed as a variation of $y = ax + b$ ($y=Fc$, $x=Fr$, $a = -1$, and $b=0$): $Fc = -Fr + 0$.

In a linear relationship among factors in a system, a change in one variable will lead to a proportionate change in the other factors. This proportionality is what ensures the straight line when the relation between the variables is plotted on an x—y axis. This kind of proportional change is the result of not having any exponential terms in the equation which would cause a disproportionality between a change in one variable and its effect on the other. Another way to state this is that, in a linear relationship, the factors are not functions of each other or mutually determining.[1] Therefore, in a linear relationship, there is a certain "independence" of each variable from the other.

---

[1] In other words, in the nonlinear logistic equation [$X_{(t+1)} = aX_t (1-X_t)$], the successive values are mutually determining since the calculation for each successive value requires a "pumping back" into the equation of the current value. This is what Feigenbaum (1983) calls functional iteration. Actually, as Stewart (1989) has pointed out, "nonlinearity" is somewhat of a misnomer since defining nonlinearity as the negation of linearity is akin to calling all animals besides elephants "nonpachyderms."

FIGURE 4.2.   SUMMARY OF LEWIN'S MODEL OF ORGANIZATIONAL CHANGE

A SYSTEM LEFT TO ITSELF NATURALLY SEEKS:	Equilibrium or resistance to change
RESISTANCE TO CHANGE IS A FUNCTION OF:	Resisting forces and "additional force-fields"
CHANGE IS:	Shift to new equilibrium level
CHANGE IS THE RESULT OF:	Imposition of an external force and "unfreezing"
WHO IS RESPONSIBLE FOR CHANGE:	The change agent(s)
THE DIRECTION OF THE CHANGE PROCESS:	External to internal
EMPHASIS IS ON:	Planning

In the case of Lewin's equilibrium equation, this linear proportionality and "independence" is shown by what happens when the forces toward change (Fc) increase: either there will be a directly proportionate but opposite increase in the forces that resist change (Fr), or the system will proportionately shift to a new equilibrium level.[2]

An important implication for OD practice is that a linear shift is conceived as the addition of a factor (to the equation) or the increase of an external force (on the social system). The shift or change is not due to any inherent potential for change in the system. Later, it will be shown that in certain ways of conceiving *nonlinear* relationships in a system, change is a potential contained in the very solution of the nonlinear equations and not the result of an imposed force.

Therefore, it is again the case that, for Lewin's way of understanding social system change, the change agent must be in a position to act *externally* on the system, getting it moving in the direction of the proposed change. (Figure 4.2 summarizes the main implications of Lewin's equilibrium-seeking and linear assumptions.)

NONEQUILIBRIUM AND NONLINEAR RESEARCH

Assumptions about equilibrium-seeking and linearity were essential to theories in nineteenth century physics aimed at explaining such mechanical systems as the steam engine (Russet, 1966; West, 1985). However, in the past 25 years a vastly different understanding has emerged from the study of such nonmechanical systems as the weather, ecology, and physiology (Crutchfield, Farmer, Packard,

---

[2] If there is a shift to a new equilibrium level, this indicates that the resultant of the two opposing forces will again be equal to zero.

& Shaw, 1986; Glass & Mackey, 1988; Gleick, 1987; Prigogine & Nicolis, 1989).

An Example of Nonlinear and Nonequilibrium System Dynamics

The Nobel Prize Winner Ilya Prigogine offers the "Benard Instability" as a simple example of nonequilibrium dynamics (Prigogine & Stengers, 1984). A liquid in a container is heated from the bottom, creating a temperature difference between the top and bottom of the container. At a critical temperature, the liquid "self-organizes"; that is, there is the sudden and startling propagation of circular, wave-like convection currents called "Benard Cells." These kinds of "self-organizing" phenomena were not studied within the context of the 19th-century equilibrium model.

The following is a summary of Nicolis's (1989) detailed analysis of the phases in the self-organization of the Benard Cells:

1. *Initial homogeneity at equilibrium*. Before the external heat source is turned on, the liquid's temperature, density and spatial structure are approximately the same throughout the liquid. This homogeneity reflects the system's equilibrium-seeking ability to eliminate temperature differences by diffusing them through the system.

2. *Application of a nonequilibrium constraint*. By creating a large enough temperature difference, the heat source can act as a nonequilibrium constraint by interfering with the system's tendency toward equilibrium. As a result, the equilibrium-seeking effect of diffusion is no longer effective in erasing temperature, density, or spatial differences.

   Schrodinger made the point that an isolated system is equivalent to a system embedded in a uniform or nonchanging environment (1968, p. 144). Since equilibrium-seeking is a dynamic of an isolated system, the implication is that a system in an *unchanging* environment will behave according to the equilibrium-seeking model. But the converse is also true: A system embedded in a *changing* environment will operate in a nonequilibrium mode. Therefore, a changing environment is equivalent to a nonequilibrium constraint.

3. *Amplification of departures from equilibrium*. Since heat lowers density, the temperature difference causes a density difference in the system with the lower density areas nearer the

source of heat. A random fluctuation or moving current in the liquid may cause a small volume of lower density liquid to displace upward. This small volume of lower density liquid will then find itself in a more dense region, and the Archimedean force will tend to *propel* or *amplify* the speed of this small volume in an upward direction. At the same time, an opposite effect may happen in the upper, colder, more dense part of the liquid: downward displacements of higher density areas will be propelled downward. The "self-organizing" convection currents of the "Benard Cells" are the result of this amplification of random fluctuations.

4. *Critical threshold and the manifestation of nonlinearity.* Before the critical temperature is reached, the relation between the elements of the system resembles the linear relations in Lewin's model examined previously. Indeed, at low temperatures, diffusion of heat is correlated in a linearly proportionate way with velocity and density change. However, this linearity is only apparent at equilibrium conditions, for when the critical threshold is reached, *nonlinear* relationships among the elements of the system are revealed.[3] The nonequilibrium constraint generated by the heat source has brought out the nonlinear effects.[4]

5. *Dissipative structures.* The self-organization that occurs in far-from-equilibrium systems are called "dissipative structures" because they dissipate or transfer energy to the environment without decomposing in the process. The organization of dissipative structures follows what Haken (1981) calls an "order parameter" —a mode of functioning of the system as a whole in which the components of the system act in a coherent and cooperative organizational pattern. Dissipative structures not only introduce a new kind of systemic order, but they also display a

---

[3] The evolution equation of the Benard system is nonlinear because "the transport of the property, like for instance, energy, is carried by the motion itself, whose velocity is one of the variables to be determined"(Nicolis, 1989, p. 330). This is the mutual-determination of factors in this kind of nonlinear relationship—they are functions of each other.

[4] An example of how the solutions of a nonlinear equation show a change or transformation is the logistic equation $X_{(t+1)} = aX_t(1 - X_t)$ (May, 1987). This equation can be expressed in feedback formulations (Goerner, 1989). The solutions of the equation traverse through different "attractors" or regimes of solutions: a fixed point attractor (the only possible attractor in a linear system), limit cycles, and "strange attractors" or "chaos").

FIGURE 4.3.   NONEQUILIBRIUM AND NONLINEAR DYNAMICS
IN SYSTEM CHANGE

1. Initial equilibrium
    — System is homogeneous, i.e., without internal differences
    — Departures from equilibrium are eliminated

2. Nonequilibrium constraint
    — Internal differences are induced
    — Equilibrium-seeking is interrupted
    — System is in contact with changing environment

3. Amplification of fluctuations
    — Random departures from equilibrium are amplified
    — Self-organization emerges

4. Nonlinearity is revealed
    — Nonequilibrium conditions release inherent nonlinearity
    — System change is result of nonlinearity emerging

5. Dissipative structures
    — New patterns of system organization
    — Adaptation of new environment

sensitivity and creative adaptation to the environment through revealing potentialities hidden in the nonlinearities of the system (Nicolis, 1989).

Figure 4.3 summarizes these principles of nonequilibrium and nonlinear dynamics.

APPLICATION OF THE NEW RESEARCH
TO ORGANIZATIONAL CHANGE

The following main points describe a nonequilibrium and nonlinear understanding of organizational change replacing Lewin's equilibrium and linear assumptions. Implications for OD practice are included with each of these nine points.

Organizational Nonlinearity Can Account for Organizational Change

Nicolis (1989) has remarked that nonlinearity in social systems may reflect processes of growth, communication, competition, or information exchange. Similarly, nonlinearity in the mixed feedback loops underlying organizational dynamics has long been a tenet of Forrester's "system dynamics" approach (1975a). Nonlinearity in social systems also shows up in other social science models: Myrdal's principle of cumulation, Merton's self-fulfilling prophecy, Bateson's cybernetics in family systems theory, and the Bounded Rationality of Herbert Simon (Richardson, 1983, pp. 7,11,12,21).[5]

At equilibrium conditions, organizations appear to behave in a fashion suggesting a linear relationship among elements in the system. But, under appropriate nonequilibrium conditions, organizational nonlinearity may lead to the kind of "self-organizing" change seen in the Benard system.[6] The point is that the nonlinearity inherent in the relationships among the elements of the system can itself account for the amplification of departures from equilibrium leading to systemic change. Nonlinearity, then, obviates the need for the imposition of an external force to overcome supposed resistance to change. Furthermore, processes which maintain stability at equilibrium can become change processes at nonequilibrium conditions —the nonlinear amplifying force is already present, but at equilibrium conditions it is manifesting in a linear fashion.

Implications for OD practice. Lewin's "force-field" diagram identifies organizational forces at equilibrium conditions, but it does not indicate nonlinearities or feedback loops expressing mutually determining relationships among the factors in a system. Therefore, force-field analysis cannot depict nonlinear potentials for change. To identify the latter, "system dynamics" diagrams can be used to show positive and negative feedback loops (Senge, 1990). Such diagrams are not for the purpose of identifying or unfreezing

---

[5] However much he may have formulated his "additional force fields" in a linear and equilibrium manner, Lewin may have had intimations of social system nonlinearity which would have shown itself in the following ways: how small changes in one factor, such as group participation, may have such a dramatic effect on system transformation; or how a system consistently finds ways to compensate for increased pressure to change.

[6] Bifurcation, marking a change in the global configuration of the organizational system, is the appearance of new physical solutions to the underlying nonlinear equations of systemic evolution (Nicolis, 1981, pp. 197, 198). From a dynamical systems perspective, this transformation is a shift in attractors (Crutchfield et al., 1986; Libchaber, 1987; Swinney, 1983; Thompson & Stewart, 1986). Attractors portray the eventual convergence of the behavior of a system into a particular pattern and express relations among system elements *independently* of the initial conditions. Each attractor is associated with at least one mode of behavior of the system: fixed point, limit cycles, or chaotic "strange attractors." By classifying attractors, insight is gained into the types of behavior a system can show over time (Goldstein, 1990).

any assumed "resistance."[7] Instead, the so-called resistance is viewed as an aspect of the nonlinearity of the system, and, therefore, it is something to be respected and worked with.[8]

If change is a natural tendency of an organization's nonlinearity, then change is something that is released at appropriate conditions, not an imposition. A system in a nonequilibrium condition will not be resisting change; it will be seeking evolution to a new way of being organized.

An Organization in Vital Contact with its Changing Environment is in a Nonequilibrium Condition

The self-organization of the Benard Cells is the result of the adaptation of the system to its changing environment. Similarly, organizations rarely dwell in unchanging environments and, to survive, organizations can't be purely isolated. Of course, organizations or work groups may be out of touch with their environments, and thus functioning as isolated systems following an equilibrium-seeking model.

But, in a nonequilibrium condition, organizations or work groups will be responsive to changes in the environment so that the nonequilibrium condition and the exchange with the environment maintain each other. Consequently, a nonequilibrium constraint is a way of describing the nonequilibrium effect on a system that is in contact with a varying environment. This nonequilibrium constraint is what establishes the system's readiness to change. It needs to be emphasized that the "environment" need not be an external environment (such as customers or market conditions): a work group is embedded in an *internal* organizational environment, and it is this internal environment that the work group must be in vital contact with.

Implication for OD Practice. Since readiness to change is a function of a system's nonequilibrium status, the change agent's role is to recognize and guide the nonequilibrium. But the change agent doesn't *change* anything—the vital environmental contact itself is the key to the change or adaptation. Therefore, there is no need for either fancy techniques of unfreezing or methods for per-

---

[7] Actually, "unfreezing" is the wrong metaphor for it refers to a phase transition—the change of ice to water which Nicolis indicates is a local intermolecular effect, not the global change seen in self-organization (1989, p. 329).

[8] For an example of how "resistance" can be viewed in this positive manner see Goldstein (1989).

suading the group to buy into the change. The group changes as it self-organizes in response to the environmental changes—its nonlinearity is activated when it is in a nonequilibrium condition.

As the mediator of a changing environment, the change agent sees to it that the environment is allowed to affect the system, as it is, without the need for persuasion or threat or manipulation. This is a more organic and less planned approach—the change agent is not conceived as facilitating change from an external source. The nonequilibrium role of the change agent is similar to what Heifetz (1988) sees as the disequilibriating effect of a good leader.

Change as the Amplification of Departures from Equilibrium

Nonlinearities enable fluctuations to be amplified and invade the whole system.[9] In far-from-equilibrium conditions, fluctuations can reach an order of magnitude where these fluctuations cannot be distinguished from macroscopic system elements (Prigogine & Stengers, 1984, p. 180). That is why these departures from equilibrium can no longer be ignored by the system. Self-organization incorporates these fluctuations or "noise" into its new way of being organized (Ciborra, Migliarese & Romano, 1984; Nonaka, 1988).

Organizational change, then, is a cooperation between chance and determinism since self-organization takes advantage of *random* fluctuations (Nicolis, 1989, p. 342). For example, by means of fluctuations, the Benard system tests several configurations and finds one (the convection cells) which can transport heat in the most effective way. In this way, the organization can take advantage of chance by using it to explore different system configurations as evolutionary, adaptive responses to environmental change (Allen, 1988, p. 120). Gemmill and Smith have proposed that for an organization to be successful in transforming itself, it needs to contain "*norms supportive of experiencing disorder and embracing it as an opportunity to experiment*" (1985, p. 762; emphasis added).

But such a perspective on departures from the norm is a very different one than is usually practiced even by OD practitioners. Most often, departures from equilibrium, including unforeseen or chance events that interfere with normal work flow are classified as unwanted noise. As a result, a great deal of thought and planning goes into how to avoid or dampen such noise in the future. As

---

[9] This is not just deviation amplification (Maruyama, 1968), for in a system dominated by equilibrium seeking, deviation-amplification will kick in a compensating equilibrium-seeking process (Forrester, 1968).

Ciborra et al. (1984) have pointed out, in the traditional under-standing of social systems, only small, reversible variety or noise is allowed and is considered subject to reequilibrating mechanisms.

Implications for OD practice. Ciborra et al. (1984) suggest that instead of ignoring it, organizational noise can be utilized in the evolutionary change of a social system, by identifying the noise and describing it in terms of its source, frequency, effects, and interdependencies. A "map" of this noise can indicate opportunities for new organizational patterns and provide a new picture of the organization's functioning which is not based solely on equilibrat-ing mechanisms.

Following this noise map, the OD practitioner can be a "non-equilibrium guide" by taking the role of supporting norms that sup-port disorder, not just equilibrium. Goldstein (1988) has proposed a method of "difference questioning" in a work group which encour-ages differentiation from the work group norms. In typical OD prac-tice, surveys are used to establish group norms and attitudes, which, during survey feedback, are presented back to the group for the member's response. These surveys are usually based on average scores, which depict group norms, not departures from group norms. To be sure, in Lewinian approaches to "action research", this kind of survey feedback can help a group move to the establish-ment of new norms. But this amounts to simply shifting from one equilibrium level to another. However, difference questioning en-courages members to state their *differing* perspectives. No attempt is made at consensus seeking—in fact, various methods may be used to further differentiate the perspectives (Goldstein, 1988).

Moreover, "difference questioning" is to be distinguished from "unfreezing."[10] Lewin's example of group participation as an in-stance of unfreezing relies on the influence of the group nexus in leading members to make decisions. This is actually an example of group pressure to conform, not amplification of departures from group norms.

Nonaka (1988) has proposed that to amplify fluctuations, an organization needs to be in a perpetual state of crisis—he quotes Canon's president Kaku: "There are two things which the top man-

---

[10] The increasing internal differences in an organizational system can also be conceptualized as the increase of information in the system. This follows from Bateson's point about information as "differences" that make a "difference" (1972). The introduction of new information into an organization by way of "difference questioning" or other techniques can be conceptualized as the internal effect of a changing environment (Goldstein, 1988; Nonaka, 1988).

agement must keep in mind in order to guarantee the continuing existence of the company. The first task . . . is to create a vision that gives meaning to the employees' jobs. The second task is to constantly convey a sense of crisis to their employees" (p. 67). This crisis is equivalent to the nonequilibrium role of the change agent to help the system take advantage of departures from equilibrium. The fact that small fluctuations have the potential of having a tremendous impact is related to the "butterfly effect" in "chaotic systems" in which small changes can have huge effects (Gleick, 1987).[11]

Organizational Change as a Natural Process of Self-organization

Self-organization is an integrated pattern of new and greater coherence, order, and complexity. At equilibrium conditions, there is no correlation, except statistical, between elements in a system (Prigogine & Stengers 1984, p.180). But nonequilibrium conditions in a nonlinear system may lead to self-organization in which " 'communication' in the system . . . keeps the coherence from being drowned out by the system's 'noise'" (Nicolis 1989, p. 340).[12]

It is important to note that the correlation that exists in self-organization is not the same as the homogeneity of a system in an equilibrium condition, which is a kind of undifferentiated enmeshment, not a correlation. Homogeneity actually reflects the lack of communication in the system since information that could be brought about by communicating is not allowed, whereas the correlation in self-organization is a correlation or communication of elements that have become differentiated from the normative mode. Self-organization is a reintegration of these departures from equilibrium into a more effective organizational pattern.

Implications for OD practice. Consensus-seeking exercises, a common tool for team-building, aim at improving communication and, hopefully, facilitating group synergy. Synergy certainly appears to be a kind of self-organization. But the question remains whether this synergy is a temporary effect of a training exercise which then needs reinforcement by various "external" buttresses or is a real case of self-organization. Synergy that emerges as work groups are allowed to experiment with departures from equilibrium in order to connect to their environment would be self-organization reflecting a real repatterning among the relationship between the elements in

---

[11] On the big effect of "small" leverage points in changing organizations see Senge (1990).

[12] For a similar phenomenon in organizations see Gemmill and Smith (1985).

FIGURE 4.4. LEWIN'S ASSUMPTIONS CONTRASTED WITH THE NEW MODEL

EQUILIBRIUM	NONEQUILIBRIUM
— systems are isolated	— systems are connected to environments
— systems tend to erase departures from equilibrium levels	— systems amplify departures from equilibrium levels
— systems resist change	— systems seek self-organization
— "refreezing" or buttressing the new equilibrium level	— dissipative structures which persist as long as environmental contact is intact

LINEARITY	NONLINEARITY
— resistance is inherent in the system	— seeds of change are inherent in the system
— change is imposed via "unfreezing"	— change is released
— change is planned	— change is organic, spontaneous, and chance is taken advantage of

the system. However, this latter type of synergy is only possible when: (a) a group is in a nonequilibrium situation, (b) the elements have broken from previous symmetries of homogeneity, and (c) chance occurrences and departures from equilibrium can be amplified and then reintegrated into new patterns which are internally generated and need no external reinforcement.

Consequently, care should be taken with consensus-seeking exercises so that they don't devolve into premature enmeshment with normative functioning being restored. In the new approach advocated here, consensus-seeking has its place but only after sufficient differentiation has taken place.

Figure 4.4 contrasts each of the above applications of the new research with Lewin's equilibrium and linear assumptions about organizational change. Figure 4.5 contrasts specific OD practices and perspectives in the new model with the Lewinian approach.

FIGURE 4.5. OD PRACTICES AND PERSPECTIVES—CONTRASTING LEWIN AND THE NEW MODEL

LEWINIAN APPROACHES	THE NEW MODEL
Survey feedback of average group norms	"Difference questioning"
Uncovering group norms	Supporting norms of disorder and nonequilibrium
Eliminating "noise"	A "noise" map
Emphasis on planning	Emphasis on chance
Overcoming resistance	Appreciating resistance
Shifting equilibrium levels	Mediating the environment and guiding nonequilibrium
Consensus-seeking	Encouraging differences
Team-building	Allowing self-organization
Big effects need big changes	Small changes can have big effects

CONCLUSION: ADVANTAGES OF THE NEW MODEL

In Lewin's model, understanding and facilitating change was tantamount to recognizing and overcoming the natural tendency of organization's to resist change. This followed from Lewin's view that organizations are primarily equilibrium-seeking systems. However, the new research recounted above suggests a radically different perspective: organizations, as primarily nonlinear systems, seek change when their environments change. The domination of a system by equilibrium-seeking dynamics represent only a partial arc in the longer-range trajectory of the system. Lewin's type of approach looks at this equilibrium-seeking phase and tries to understand change as a sequence of these partial phases. But this sequence cannot explain the type of restructuring and reordering that occurs in self-organization.

Since environments of an organization are rarely uniform, equilibrium conditions are also rare—more common would be the effect of changing environments acting as nonequilibrium constraints.

In an equilibrium model, the locus of change must be external (Sorokin, 1941, pp. 691, 692). This suggests that the system lacks its own inner resources for transformation or development. In the new model, the forces for change are already inherent in the system. Therefore, external imposition by means of "unfreezing" and "refreezing" are not what facilitates change. Instead, change is revealed and released as the system adapts to its environment. The change agent helps guide the nonequilibrium condition that results when a system is in vital contact with its environment. Because nonlinearity can amplify small changes, the new approach takes advantage of chance and diversity: organizational "random noise" is no longer something to dampen; it can be a source of creative change.

REFERENCES

Abraham, R., & Shaw, C. (1984). *Dynamics: The geometry of behavior, part one: Periodic behavior*. Santa Cruz, CA: Aerial Press.

Allen, P. (1988). Dynamic models of evolving systems. *System Dynamics Review, 4* (1,2), 109–130.

Bateson, G. (1972). *Steps to an ecology of mind*. New York: Ballantine Books.

Berge, P., Pomeau, I., & Vidal, C. (1984). *Order within chaos: Towards a deterministic approach to turbulence*. New York: Wiley.

Burke, W. (1987). *Organization development: A normative view*. Reading, MA: Addison-Wesley.

Ciborra, C., Migliarese, P., & Romano, P. (1984). A methodological inquiry of organizational noise in sociotechnical systems. *Human Relations*, 37(8), 565–588.

Coch, L., & French, J. (1978). Overcoming resistance to change. In W. Natemeyer (Ed.), *Classics of Organizational Behavior* (pp. 300–318). Oak Park, IL: Moore.

Crutchfield, J., Farmer, J., Packard, N., & Shaw, S. (1986, December). Chaos. *Scientific American*, 6 (255), 46–57.

Feigenbaum, M. (1978). Quantitative universality for a class of nonlinear transformations. *Journal of Statistical Physics 19*, 25–52.

Forrester, J. W. (1968). *Principles of Systems*. Cambridge, MA: MIT Press.

Forrester, J. W. (1975a). Common foundations underlying engineering and management. In *The Collected Papers of J.W. Forrester* (pp. 61–80). Cambridge, MA: Wright-Allen Press.

Forrester, J. W. (1975b). Counterintuitive behavior of social systems. In *The collected papers of J.W. Forrester* (pp. 211–244). Cambridge, MA: Wright-Allen Press.

Gemmill, G. & Smith, C. (1985). A Dissipative Structure Model of Organization Transformation, *Human Relations, 38*(8), 751–766.

Glass, L. and Mackey, M. (1988). *From clocks to chaos: The rhythms of life*. Princeton, NJ: Princeton University Press.

Gleick, J. (1987). *Chaos: The making of a new science*. New York: Viking Press.

Goerner, S. (1989). *Chaos and Eastern thinking*. San Francisco: Saybrook Institute.

Goldstein, J. (1988). A far-from-equilibrium systems approach to resistance to change. *Organizational Dynamics, 17*(2), 16–26.

Goldstein, J. (1989). The affirmative core of resistance. *The Organization Development Journal, 7*(1), 32–38.

Goldstein, J. (1990). A nonequilibrium, nonlinear approach to organizational change. *Systems Dynamics '90, 1*, 425–439. (Proceedings of the 1990 International System Dynamics Conference).

Haken, H. (1981). *The science of structure: Synergetics*. New York: Van Nostrand Reinhold.

Heifetz, R. (1988). Face to Face: Interview, *Inc, 10*(10), 36–48.

Lewin, K. (1948). *Resolving social conflict: Selected Papers on group dynamics*. New York: Harper & Row.

Lewin, K. (1951). *Field theory in social science*. New York: Harper & Row.

Libchaber, A. (1987). From Chaos to turbulence in Benard convection. M. Berry, I. Percival, & N. Weiss (Eds.), In *Dynamical chaos*. Princeton, NJ: Princeton University Press.

Maruyama, M. (1968). The second cybernetics: Deviation-amplifying mutual causal processes. In W. Buckley (Ed.), *Modern systems research for the behavioral scientist* (pp. 304–316) Chicago: Aldine.

May, R. M. (1987). Chaos and the dynamics of biolgoical populations. In M. Berry, I. Percival, & N. Weiss (Eds.), *Dynamical chaos* Princeton, NJ: Princeton University Press.

Morgan, G. (1986). *Images of organization*. Beverly Hills: Sage.

Nicolis, G. (1981). Bifurcations, fluctuations, and dissipative structures. In R. Enns, B. Jones, R. Miura, & S. Rangnekar *Nonlinear phenomena in physics and biology*, NY: Plenus Press.

Nicolis, G. (1989). Physics of far-from-equilibrium systems and self-organization. In P. W. Davies (Ed.), *The new physics*. Cambridge, England: Cambridge University Press.

Nonaka, I. (1988). Creating organizational order out of chaos: Self-renewal in Japanese firms. *California Management Review, 30*(3), 57–73.

Prigogine, I., & Stengers, I. (1984). *Order out of chaos: Man's new dialogue with nature*. New York: Bantam Books.

Prigogine, I., & Nicolis, G. (1989). *Exploring complexity*. New York: W.H. Freeman.

Richardson, G. (1983, July). *The feedback concept in American social science with implications for system dynamics*. System Dynamics Group Paper #D-3417, presented at the International System Dynamics Conference.

Russett, C. (1966). *The concept of equilibrium in American social thought*. New Haven, CT: Yale University Press.

Schrodinger, E. (1968), Order, disorder, and entropy. In W. Buckley (Ed.), *Modern Systems Research for the Behavioral Scientist*. Chicago: Aldine. (pp. 143–146).

Senge, P. (1990). *The fifth discipline: The art and practice of the learning organization*. New York: Doubleday.

Sorokin, P. (1941). *Social and cultural dynamics* (Vol. 4). New York: American Book Company.

Stewart, I. (1989). *Does God play dice: The mathematics of chaos*. Oxford: Basil Blackwell.

Swinney, H. L. (1983). Observations of order and chaos in nonlinear systems. In D. Campbell & H. Rose (Eds.), *Order in chaos*. Amsterdam: North-Holland.

Thompson, J. & Stewart, H. (1986). *Nonlinear dynamics and chaos*. New York: Wiley.

West, B. (1985). *An essay on the importance of being nonlinear*. Berlin: Springer-Verlag.

5

Some Issues in the Adaptation of Organization and Management Methods to Contrasting Countries, Cultures, and Societies: Reflections from Hungary

Imre Lövey

I would like to begin this chapter with some personal background information to show why I am particularly interested in this topic. I was one of the first to study and introduce Organizational Development (OD) and an experiential type of management training in Hungary, and perhaps in Eastern Europe as well, in the late 1970s.

I became involved in this U.S.-originated approach through a UNIDO (United Nations Industrial Development Organization) project, which was led by an expert from India who had worked in the United States for four years. In this way, I experienced a kind of cultural, social and economic variety from the very beginning, which later included professional visits to several countries in the East and West.

Since I entered this field of study, many colleagues and friends (both foreigners and Hungarians) have asked if these methods would work in my country. These challenges made me think a great deal about the adaptability of the different training and development methodologies to other cultures and societies.

In this chapter I would like to share my understanding about these issues based on my own experience, including successes and failures alike.

One way to approach this is to look first at the steps involved in adapting a new method:

1. Understanding the essence of the method and the circumstances within which it has been developed.
2. Analyzing and comparing the basic factors in the two cultures,

societies and economies which are essential for the applicability of the method.

3. Making decisions about the implementation of the method, including the necessary modifications, timing, resources, and so on.

In the following I will use the case of the adaptation of OD to Hungary as an example for this process. After a brief review of Step 1 most of the chapter will be devoted to Step 2, which is the core issue. Finally, some of the traps of decision making in the implementation stage will be discussed.

THE CIRCUMSTANCES OF THE DEVELOPMENT OF OD AND ITS ESSENCE

Of all the background factors facilitating the development of OD in the United States, the following three may be considered to be of primary importance:

1. Organizational Development (OD) evolved in a market-oriented, highly competitive economic environment, where all the methods which could improve efficiency and management of a business were greatly appreciated. If a method is generally believed to contribute to the achievement of the above-mentioned aims, it is likely to become widespread throughout business life.

2. The results of research in the social sciences were naturally incorporated in the everyday life of a society with a pragmatic approach such as that of the United States as early as in the decades preceding World War II (take, for example, the experiments of Elton Mayo in Hawthorn and the spread of the Human Relation trend).

    After World War II, general research in sociopsychology and the specific findings concerning group dynamics (e.g., Kurt Lewin's 1947 T-group results) opened up new perspectives in the application of these results to solving organizational problems.

3. The student movements of the 1960s and the popularity of the hippie values, especially among the young, signaled that in the field of material values versus human values the significance of the latter had increased considerably in the society. This tendency influenced the internal lives of the various companies, institutions and other organizations as well. The significance

attached to the manifold ways of developing human potential increased. This was accompanied by the widespread improvement of general economic well-being, which consequently increased the significance of social needs and their satisfaction beyond the realm of basic material needs and a sense of security.

The simultaneous presence of all these conditions made the foundation and widespread acceptance of organizational development possible.

COMPARATIVE ANALYSIS OF THE BACKGROUND FACTORS NECESSARY FOR THE ADAPTABILITY OF OD

As far as the adaptability of OD is concerned, the last 40 years of Hungarian history provided an excellent opportunity to examine the circumstances under which OD methods could not be used and the circumstances under which OD could be accepted and applied. To do this it is worth separating the socioeconomic circumstances of the completely rigid, orthodox central planning system of the 1950s and 1960s from the increasingly more open liberalism and market orientation of the 1970s and 1980s, even if the latter have their limitations.

Four basic factors in the external circumstances affect the applicability of OD in a country, culture, economy, or society:

1. Organization's need for a substantial level of independence
2. External pressure on organization for continuous renewal and development
3. Advanced level of social sciences
4. Belief in basic human values such as democracy, tolerance, openness, trust, and participation.

In the following these factors will be reviewed in detail, separating Hungary into two distinct periods.

Independence of Organizations

Organizations need a substantial level of independence to make decisions about important issues concerning their present and future. In other words, they have to feel that they are in charge of their fate, that it is under their control. In a private economy this is more or less taken for granted, but in a socialist one this is definitely not so.

Centralized economy. In centrally planned economies there is a strong belief that the operation of the whole society is optimal if everything is planned centrally by the government, if the exact figures of production, plans, investment, compensation, and so on, are given to the companies and all they have to do is to do their job and meet these figures. This centralized direction of the economy is necessarily accompanied by a strongly authoritarian style of leadership and organizational culture. There is no need for independent initiative coming from lower levels. What is more, this is even functional, since the aim is to follow the instructions coming from the top in the closest possible way.

Under this system in Hungary, the various ministries carefully prescribed everything for the companies and institutions belonging to them, including the appointment of managers of key importance. Profit-making companies were deprived of their profits so that losing companies could be supported, but all this was of little importance, since prices had nothing to do with market value and production costs. Naturally the companies, or rather their managers, had no sense of independence; they did not feel that their company's development and its future depended on them. They devoted their energy to building up good personal contacts with the leading authorities rather than to finding ways to increase the efficiency of their organization, since the future of both the individual and the organization depended much more on the former than on the latter.

Economic regulations. The new economic mechanism introduced in 1968 gradually, albeit with frequent lapses, decreased the direct control of the ministries. Instead, it attempted to influence companies with indirect methods such as economic regulations. Profit-making organizations could, for example, retain a portion of their profit for themselves and they could spend it on financing investments and on increasing the income of the managers and the staff.

Thus two important changes took place:

- independence in decision making for the companies and their managers began to evolve, and
- a direct material interest in a more efficient and profitable operation began to take shape. (However, both were limited and differed in degree within the given period.)

Under such circumstances, companies began to take an interest in discovering methods that could help them in operating their organizations more successfully and efficiently. One of these methods was organizational development.

The case of one of our client companies whom we have been advising on OD for years illustrates the above-mentioned process of change. This company belongs to an industry that faces hardships worldwide, and it too felt the effects more and more.

They asked for our help in order to solve their problems. The organizational diagnosis and the managers' workshops clearly pointed to the fact that the company would not progress without cleaning up its profile and concentrating its energies in fewer directions. In order to improve the cooperation among the departments and to encourage more responsibility and initiative on the part of individuals, a simpler and more decentralized structure had to be established. In order to achieve this, it would have been necessary to phase out a number of activities. However, the company was unable to make important changes in this field for many years because rules set by the ministry did not allow them to. For example, this company could not cease one of its activities because it was delivering to the army and to the state railway system and the ministry obliged them to continue this at a price set by the ministry.

It was difficult to motivate the leaders to open up possibilities for changes and development that depended on them as long as external ties and direct interference with the management of the company had a major impact on the company's achievements. A major part of the time in workshops organized for them was spent in complaining about their lack of independence. Even though in the end they judged that each OD intervention was useful and they even asked for newer ones, they did not carry through their decisions consistently because upon returning to their work they felt that they had no impact on basic matters. When from one year to the next the direct interference in the company's basic internal affairs on the part of the ministry ceased to exist—for example, they no longer appointed the senior management and did not force delivery to the army—the changes planned for years took place quickly as part of an OD process: the senior management finalized the product strategy with the midlevel management participating in the decision-making process; they stopped certain activities while emphasizing others; they formed independent profit centers from separate departments; and they clarified the conditions for cooperation and the mechanism for resolving conflicts.

The next year, the company, for the first time in many years, made a profit and increased the wages of its employees substantially.

External Pressure on Organizations for Continuous Renewal and Development

This pressure can take the form of a competitive market. In this situation organizations have a real need for methods which could promote their development.

Shortage-based economics. During the era of rigorous central planning, all the products, buyers, and suppliers were centrally designated. No competition or real pressure to provide quality products and services existed. This was a comparatively safe but low-achieving system. No real incentive for renewal and development existed for the organizations working within these circumstances. The East-European automobile industry is a good, albeit sad, example of this. The same models may be manufactured for 20 or 30 years, and even though they do not come up to modern standards (e.g., mileage, environmental protection, safety, etc.), one still has to wait several years to buy them. In these shortage-based economies, companies could sell everything they produced regardless of the quality. Under these conditions companies were not particularly eager to look for new methodologies for improvement.

After economic reform. The external circumstances mentioned above gradually began to change in Hungary after the economic reform. This was especially true of companies selling their products on the world market.

The need for renewal and development emerged at more and more companies during this period, but since most of them enjoyed a monopolistic position in the domestic market (as many of them still do), they made only partial efforts to apply various methods that could help their renewal. Since most organizations were not under really drastic external pressure, numerous half-finished, dead, or superficial experiments in organization development were carried out during this period as well.

Radical change in this field has only taken place in the last couple of years in Hungary, since concrete evidence has been provided that the government will not offer a helping hand to every money-losing company. And in the future it will have even fewer financial resources to subsidize such organizations. Thus, companies and institutions are increasingly forced to make their activity more efficient and profitable in Hungary today. This tendency is emphasized by the fact that there is a growing pressure for their products and services to compete on the world market. Under the influence of these imperative circumstances they are more and more willing to adopt methodologies which could contribute to improving their standards and efficiency.

These dramatic changes are clearly reflected in my colleagues' and my own experience in consulting over the past ten years. Some years ago our work in organizational development progressed very slowly and it was difficult to come up with concrete and tangible results. Summing up this period, one could say that companies felt the need for change—they even made some limited efforts to this end—but serious commitments were never made as they were not really forced to undertake the inconvenience and difficulties that accompany essential changes. From the perspective of the OD consultants, there seemed to have been a great number of individually successful, highly appreciated interventions and OD actions led by them; still, all in all, no essential changes took place within the organizations.

Recently, with bankruptcy as a real danger to companies and at the same time the possibility of sudden positive advance being much more a reality (e.g., by establishing joint ventures), the importance of the work of professional OD experts has been significantly upgraded. Top managers of companies will devote considerable time, energy and, of course, money to the OD process if they see hope that with its help they will find a way out of their difficulties and/or will increase their competitiveness.

Most major Hungarian companies serve as examples to support this point. The case of one of my current clients could be called typical, too. For decades, this company had a monopolistic position in building and renovating public buildings in Budapest (hotels, theaters, hospitals, etc.). The customers stood in line waiting many years for their turn. Their bargaining position in the question of price was weak and they had to put up with missed completion deadlines and other insufficiencies.

In these circumstances it was understandable that the company relaxed; it operated a huge bureaucratic center with a strictly centralized decision-making process and management style. Through their good personal relations with the main authorities, the directors arranged all the orders and other necessary things for the company.

The employees of the company grumbled and expressed their dissatisfaction with their lack of independence stemming from the overcentralized structure and the low level of efficiency; however, the company made a profit, paid relatively well and secured the construction of the most exciting buildings from a professional standpoint for its employees. Under these circumstances, no important changes happened at this company until recently. At this point the senior management considered implementing basic changes. The main reasons for this decision were the following:

- They no longer enjoyed a monopoly in this field because not only were they allowed to build public buildings but any other competitor could submit plans.
- Austrian construction companies who provided faster service and better quality work appeared in the hotel construction field.
- Their prices at competitive biddings proved to be too high in comparison to the competition; even though their professional qualifications and their experience were appreciated, their prices were still considered too high and they won fewer and fewer commissions.
- The best employees went to work for the competition where they were offered higher salaries.
- Because of the above-mentioned, the voices demanding greater autonomy for the employees and for certain departments and changes within the company got louder.

This was the situation when the senior management turned to OD professionals for help. After interviews to assess the situation, a three-day (large-group) workshop was held, involving all three levels of upper, midlevel, and lower management. During the workshop, they analyzed the company's situation, formulated a vision for the future, and set down guidelines for change in organizational structure and culture.

I think the essence of this subsection holds true for countries outside Eastern Europe as well. The automobile industry of the United States—take the Ford company for example—followed a similar course in the 1960s, 1970s, and 1980s, when their relatively comfortable position on the market was replaced by a very critical situation due to the oil crisis and the Japanese challenge. The way out was found by a management with a new approach.

Acceptance of the Social Sciences

Since a major pillar of OD is the use of the theory and techniques of applied behavioral science, it is very important to have an advanced level of social sciences such as sociology, psychology, and socio-psychology in the culture, country, economy, or society concerned.

After World War II. With the Stalinist system coming into power in Hungary, these sciences were denounced as the "remnants of capitalism" and as such, were persecuted. They practically disappeared from the culture of the country and generations grew up while these sciences were considered taboo.

This gap of approximately two decades considerably retarded the whole profession and the development of these sciences, and left its mark on the thinking of the public for a long time. People, including managers as well, talked about psychology and sociology with suspicion, sarcasm, and distrust. They openly declared that these were not sciences, and they did not believe in them at all. These views live on in many people even today.

Naturally, with this kind of attitude, OD, which actively relies on these disciplines, were not enthusiastically embraced, and the experts representing it were automatically considered *persona non grata* in the organizations.

The 1960s—1980s. In the second half of the 1960s these disciplines slowly began to seep back into the world of legitimate sciences and departments began to be formed for them at the universities. Still, long years had to pass before the public began to forget its prejudices and to take these fields seriously.

When, at the end of the 1970s, with some of my friends I started management training courses based on experiential learning, our colleagues unanimously claimed that it would simply not work in Hungary. Fortunately, all this belongs to the past now. The news that these programs were useful, new and interesting quickly spread, and perhaps these training courses have contributed to the fact that the public is more open towards these fields of social sciences and they are beginning to receive the recognition they deserve.

By the end of the 1980s we reached the point where, compared with other organizational methods, OD had no particular disadvantage because it involved sciences which used to be regarded as "untouchable."

Widespread Acceptance and Belief in Basic Human Values such as Democracy, Tolerance, Openness, Trust and Participation

This is a factor which, admitting some exaggeration, automatically divides the organizations of a country into two groups: Those in the first group are potential clients for OD, while those in the second do not believe in these kinds of things. With a value-oriented approach like OD this is quite natural.

These values, though, may be true not only for organizations but countries as well. The value system influencing the everyday life of a whole country may naturally dominate the inner lives of the different organizations, too. In Hungary, at least, this was the case.

1950s Hungary. Hungary was a classic example of a police state where the above values were not only missing, but their opposites prevailed day to day. The system was so antidemocratic and intolerant that if anybody announced this fact aloud, he could easily find himself in prison. Personnel departments were in fact outposts of the state security authorities (KGB).

I think no further explanation is needed as to why this was not a world open to OD.

Conditions for democracy. One of the positive results of the system created by János Kádár, who was the head of Hungary for over 30 years, is that following the 1950s the clutches of the police state eased considerably compared to the conditions in the rest of Eastern Europe. In more and more issues, people slowly began to get used to being able to voice opinions different from the official ones.

By the 1980s such generations came to maturity, whose minds had not been directly influenced by the paranoid, despotic world of the 1950s. Many of them were in their most receptive years in the second half of the 1960s or at the beginning of the 1970s. This was the era of the beat generation and of rebellious youth in Hungary as well. This generation experienced early on that it did not have to obey unconditionally the commands of authority, that new ways could be tried out and people's fate could be actively shaped.

The conditions needed for this to become reality, however, began to exist only at the end of the 1980s. The provision of conditions needed for democracy, tolerance, human values and initiative to evolve were included in the programs of the government at this time. The elderly, "good comrade" managers, who were used to an authoritarian system of direction, were more and more often replaced by the representatives of the above-mentioned manager-minded generation with a more open and democratic way of thinking. These external circumstances, which are decisive factors for organizations, and the generation change in the management companies both contributed to the creation of an environment receptive to the OD type of approach and value system.

Summary

An examination of the four factors listed in this section is indispensable in Eastern Europe if an OD type of approach is to be introduced.

Having consulted with colleagues from Eastern Europe, my experience is that the conclusion of the above comparative analysis concerning the two periods of Hungary may be useful in determining how successful organizational development could be promoted in the various post-socialist countries.

TRAPS TO BE AVOIDED WHEN ADAPTING
OD TYPE OF APPROACHES

The overall methodology of OD and especially the micro methods concentrating primarily on the individual and on small groups are based on general rules of personality psychology, sociopsychology and group dynamics which hold true for communities open to OD in countries, societies, economies, and cultures of the greatest variety. Transaction Analysis is a good example of this. It is successfully used as a theoretical framework in the United States, in Hungary, and in India (Jaeger, 1986). And colleagues in the United States, Germany, Japan, India, and Hungary, to name just a few, have led successful T-groups, which have similar group dynamics (Massarik, 1964, 1982).

Given proper professional training and cross-cultural sensitivity, these micro-level interventions, based on some universal rules, can quite probably achieve considerable success in a short period of time.

The export procedure of these programs is the following: The "guru," coming in most cases from a developed western country, leads some short or long programs, the success of which is enhanced by its novelty; then, amidst praises, he will leave the country which intends to adapt these methods.

When the participants get beyond the euphoria of these first programs, and they attempt to apply the experience they gained in the micro programs within an organization which is limited in action by the given external circumstances, the sobering reality of unchanged circumstances has to be faced in most cases, and what remains from the planned changes is merely nostalgia.

Experts from abroad may get positive reinforcement concerning the adaptability of the new method, from the fact that OD micro methods do work in the new circumstances, and from the fact that they may run into numerous "acquaintances" in the inner dynamics of the organizations. Examples of these are the dynamics of the relationships between the various organizational groups, and the dynamics of cooperation and competition, including power games for gaining control over various resources and conflict situations and their effect. For instance, the tension between R & D, production, sales, and finance is characteristic for production organizations from all parts of the globe.

It is true that in addition to the similarities mentioned above, there are many essential and readily perceivable differences in the culture and social customs of the various countries (see, e.g., Hofstede's research results, Hofstede, 1980); still, that should not present an insurmountable obstacle for an OD expert with the necessary sensitivity and openness. An OD consultant possessing considerable consulting practice will meet extremely different organizational cultures, standards in behavior, and personalities within a given country or culture. One of the most important elements of his profession is merely unprejudiced openness in observing the events in a given organization.

It is not by chance that the traits considered to be important for a consultant working in an alien culture are similar to those which are generally necessary for a good OD consultant:

- awareness of his or her own culture, values and beliefs
- empathy
- avoidance of judging or labeling
- ability to learn from experience and to adapt him/herself
- tolerance of uncertainty
- persistence
- high degree of self-understanding.

According to all this, an expert attempting to do OD type of work in a foreign country will quite possibly find enough similarities on the individual, group, and organizational levels to come to the conclusion that if something worked at home, it will work with the necessary adjustments here as well. As has been mentioned above, he/she is very likely to get quick and positive reinforcement in the form of feedback. The question arises: Does this actually mean that in the long run OD will contribute to the more efficient and successful work of the organizations in the given country?

The answer is: not necessarily. According to the summary given in the second section it can be stated that if we want to get a realistic estimate of the long-term effect of OD actions, we must not ignore the system external conditions existing in the given country, society and economy. It is no accident that of all the programs offered in a series by the OD Network in Hungary the one raising the greatest interest was titled "Successful Interventions, Training Courses— Unsuccessful Organizational Development."

Just as a conscientious OD consultant will find out before taking on an assignment whether the conditions of the organization are conducive to successful organizational development, so must he objectively assess to what extent the external conditions which are absolutely essential for OD to bring long-term results and to gain ground in that country are present before he attempts to apply them.

Unfortunately, the subjective conditions needed for this objective preliminary study cannot be easily established either by the OD experts coming from abroad, or by their colleagues from the given country. The factors liable to hinder an objective and detailed analysis of the situation are as follows:

1. The perspective of OD experts usually extends to the dimensions of individuals, groups and organizations. They tend to have less experience in reviewing the main features characterizing a country or society. In most cases this is outside their scope of attention and they may not realize that for the sake of the success of OD this wider context has to be taken into consideration as well.

2. Applied behavioral sciences are of primary importance in OD. Consequently, such economic issues as economic management or systems of regulation lie in most cases outside the field of interest of OD people, so they are less likely to consider their effect on the organization. However, they may be of crucial importance. (See subsections on economic regulation and economic reform.)

3. Both the expert coming from abroad and his colleague in the given country usually have an overriding personal interest in introducing OD (in getting the business or requiring the method) to be able to assess the facts in a truly unbiased way.

4. On the micro level, numerous similarities can be discovered which reinforce the adaptability of OD methods. Because of this, overall questions are often not raised. The real issue is not the adaptability of each methodological technique but rather whether these can be put together in a system which is able to increase the efficiency and productivity of the organization within the social, economic, and cultural conditions of the given society.

In order to be able to avoid distortions when making important decisions regarding the adaptation of OD activities and the development of local professional competence, a thorough analysis of the situation is necessary. This should examine both the essence of the method to be adapted and the external social, economic, and cultural conditions under which this approach can be successfully applied. This information has to be compared with the local conditions and then the decision can be made.

In the question of adaptation, the starting point should never be one particular technique but the understanding and comparison of both the essence of the approach and the specific features of the receiving medium. In this way mere automatic copying of a method alien to the culture of the given country can be avoided. Instead, the result will be an approach which will fit in well with and which can be effectively applied to the given culture.

REFERENCES

Adler, N. J., & Campbell, N. (1989). In search of appropriate methodology: From outside the People's Republic of China looking in. *Journal of International Business Studies, 20*(1), 61–74.

Hofstede, G. (1980). *Culture's consequences: International differences in work related values.* Beverly Hills, CA: Sage Publications.

Jaeger, A. M. (1986). Organization development and national culture: Where's the fit? *Academic of Management Review, 11*(1), 178–190.

Lewin, K. (1948). *Resolving social conflicts.* New York: Harper Row.

Massarik, F. (1964–65). Saying what you feel—Reflections on Personal Openness in Japan. *International Understanding,* v. *2*(1), 26–33.

Massarik, F. (1982). Small group training and the T-group in Asia: A re-examination. In *G. Fatzer (Ed.), Organisations.* Zurich.

Pearce, J. L. (1989). *Socialism to capitalism: Preliminary observations on Hungarian organizational behavior.* Unpublished Manuscript, International Management Center, Budapest, Hungary.

Tainio, R., & Santalainen, T. (1984). Some evidence for the culture relativity of organizational development programs. *The Journal of Applied Behavioral Science, 20*(2), 93–111.

6

In Search of Existence:
On the Use of the Existential
Tradition in Management
and Organization Development*

Thierry (Terry) C. Pauchant
Associate Professor of Management
Ecole des Hautes Etudes Commerciales (HEC)
University of Montréal, Canada

Let us consider this waiter in the cafe. His movement is quick and forward, a little too precise, a little too rapid. He comes toward the patrons with a step a little too quick. He bends forward a little too eagerly; his voice, his eyes express an interest a little too solicitous for the order of the customer. . . . All his behavior seems to us a game. . . . He is playing, he is amusing himself. . . . He is playing at being a waiter in a cafe . . . the waiter in the cafe plays with his condition in order to realize it. This obligation is not different from that which is imposed on all tradesmen. Their condition is wholly of ceremony. . . . There is the dance of the grocer, of the tailor, of the auctioneer, by which they endeavor to persuade their clientele that they are nothing but a grocer, an auctioneer, a tailor. . . . A grocer who dreams is offensive to the buyer, because such a grocer is not wholly grocer. . . . There are indeed many precautions to imprison a man in what he is, as if he lived in perpetual fear that he might escape from it, that he might break away and suddenly elude his condition. (Sartre, 1966, pp. 100-101)

Being the dominant cultural value, competitive success is likewise the dominant criterion for self-valuation; it is accepted as the means for validating the self in one own's eyes as well as in the eyes of others. Whatever threatens this goal is, therefore, the occasion for profound anxiety for the individual in our culture because the threat is to values held essential to one's existence as a personality. (May, 1950, p. 206)

*I would like to thank Omar Aktouf, Dorinda Cavanaugh, Fred Massarik, Estelle Morin, and Didier Van Den Hove for their helpful comments on previous drafts of this chapter.

They were offered the choice between becoming kings or the courier of kings. The way children would, they all wanted to be couriers. There-fore they are only couriers who hurry about the world, shouting to each other—since there are no kings—messages that have become meaningless. They would like to put an end to this miserable life of theirs but they dare not because of their oaths of service. (Kafka, 1961, p. 175)

I'm a Budman . . . I know who I am. I'm a Budman . . . This Bud's for you. Budweiser Company. (*Radio advertisement*)

The basic theme of this chapter is that some current problems facing individuals, organizations, and society are existential in na-ture and thus need to be addressed in existential terms. In this chapter, I consider some of the means by which individuals, partic-ularly as members of organizations, have attempted to resolve these issues, but suggest that indeed these attempts themselves have exacerbated the problems. In particular, I suggest that while the popular trend in the "search for excellence" derives from the existen-tial tradition, the fragmented use of this tradition has had, on the whole, a perverse effect. For example, the "search for excellence" has only emphasized limited parts of the essential argument. Substan-tially, it appears that there is a need for more informed use of the existential tradition, based on scientific debate in existential philos-ophy, psychology, and literature, with a focus on the development of the modern organization.

EXISTENTIAL ISSUES IN CONTEMPORARY SOCIETY AND ORGANIZATIONS

The existential tradition points to two interrelated human experi-ences. First, it notes the paramount importance of the concept of *identity*, viewing the conduct of human affairs *as based on the subjective and personal experience* of individuals. As such, exis-tentialists consider the nature of human suffering involved with change in general. In this perspective, the experience of change, including organizational change efforts, often triggers in individu-als a flood of threatening concerns, such as a loss of life meaning, a sense of inner desperation, a sense that the "ground has been pulled from under one's feet," or the experience of deep anxiety. In the organizational domain, a small number of authors have argued that the field of organizational development at large has not so far given sufficient recognition to the significance of these existential issues, and instead has addressed only the manifest character of change itself (McWhinney, 1980; 1992; Tannenbaum & Hanna, 1985; Schein, 1990).

Second, the existential tradition points to the necessity for human beings *to fully realize the meaning of their own mortality*, that is, both biological and "symbolic death." On the positive side, this realization allows individuals to become more genuinely alive, more conscious of their need to deny this reality of death, and thus affirming life. On a less positive note, this more authentic way can also trigger anguishing reflection on life's meaning, its potential absurdity, and the human capacity to change this condition.

While the existential tradition points to these two basic human experiences, to attempt to rigorously define what constitutes "existentialism" is elusive. As noted by Friedman (1964) or Kauffman (1956), for example, existentialism is not a precisely defined field of knowledge. Rather it is a "mood," the starting point of this mood being the search for human "authenticity." Overall, existentialists insist on the necessity for humans to be "involved," "real," embracing life "fully," in its most wonderful, life-enhancing aspects, as well as in its most terrifying or anguishing ones. In this sense, the existential tradition is primarily a quest for subjective and personal meaning. Thus, existentialists are primarily concerned with how individuals might consciously live their lives, based on the acceptance of their own death and the realization of the potential richness and mystery of life.

Yet, existentialists themselves are divided on the nature and the source of this "meaning." Some, such as Buber (1958) or Ortega y Gasset (1958) stress that individuals can only develop this meaning through the finding of their true "essence," "predetermined" purpose, or "vocation". Others, such as Bugental (1988) or Rogers (1980), see this meaning as springing from the "core self" of individuals, the core of their personality, their "true center." Still others, such as Heidegger (1963), Kierkegaard (1941) or Rank (1961) argue for the need for going "beyond the self," stressing that inner meaning is only realized from the "very ground of creation," the "transpersonal" or the "spiritual realm". Or Sartre (1943) and Camus (1951), insisted that individuals can only develop meaning through acting in the world—creating through their own existence and actions their own essence.

While existentialists disagree on the source of this meaning, they do agree, that in the absence of its realization, individuals experience anxiety, despair, or boredom. Indeed, these authors insist that the most crucial problem currently confronting human beings is the profound difficulty of finding and actualizing this meaning. For example, Becker has argued that "the crisis of modern society is precisely that the youth no longer feel heroic in the plan for action that their culture has set up" (Becker, 1973, p. 6). Sartre has advanced the concept of "bad faith" in which individuals attempt to escape despair by embracing a set of roles and tasks through which they (in an illusive manner) "define" themselves (Sartre, 1966). Heidegger has stressed the issue of "self-estrangement" (Heidegger, 1963). Bakan spoke of the despair of "epistemological loneliness" (Bakan, in May, Angel, & Ellenberger, 1958); and Nietzsche proposed that the disease of contemporary human beings is the "soul gone stale" (Nietzsche, 1973). In the same vein, Maslow spoke of a "sickness of the soul" when self-actualization needs cannot be met (Maslow, 1971, p. 44).

Modern existential psychology and psychoanalysis have discussed these subjective experiences of despair and anxiety, and resulting disorders such as depressive psychosis or schizophrenia (Hoeller, 1990). May, for example, has argued that anxiety "is not an affect among other affects such as pleasure or sadness," but rather an "ontological characteristic of man," being "the experience of the threat of imminent non-being" (May et al., 1958, p. 50). In this sense, anxiety is not "objectified" as is fear, but is rather experienced from "all sides at once," being a subjective state of individuals realizing that they can be "destroyed," that their experience as a "self" can disappear, that they can die "symbolically" or "physically," or that their lives are without substance, "deathlike," "flat." In the school of Self Psychology this negative experience is described as an overall sense of not being "real," or of not being "there," an experience of "inner emptiness," a lack of purpose and direction, a sense of "falling apart," a lack of "zest" or joy in life, a sense of fragmentation, an experience of futility and boredom, a sense of separation from society and the community, a sense of alienation from one's life and work, an anguish about "disappearing" or becoming "invisible," a lack of focus, or a sense of anxiety about one's future (Kohut, 1971, 1984; Pauchant & Mitroff, 1992. For a similar list, see also Maslow's "metapathologies," 1971, p. 317).

Perhaps it is the literary work in existentialism that best expresses this experience of anguish, despair, and boredom. I present below two quotes, respectively from Hesse and Sartre, the first pointing to an experience of "symbolic death," and the second pointing to the realization of "physical death:"

> There is much to be said for contentment and painlessness, for these
> bearable and submissive days, on which neither pain nor pleasure is

audible, but pass by whispering and on tip-toe. But the worst of it is that it is just this contentment that I cannot endure. After a short while it fills me with irrepressible hatred and nausea. In desperation I have to escape and throw myself on the road to pleasure, or, if that cannot be, on the road to pain. When I have neither pleasure nor pain and have been breathing for a while the lukewarm insipid air of these so-called good and tolerable days, I feel so bad in my childish soul that I smash my moldering lyre of thanksgiving in the face of the slumbering god of contentment and would rather feel the very devil burn in me than this warmth of a well-heated room. A wild longing for strong emotions and sensations seethes in me, a rage against this toneless, flat, normal and sterile life. (Hesse, 1963, p. 31).

"It's like a nightmare," Tom was saying. "You want to think something, you always have the impression that it's all right, that you're going to understand and then it slips, it escapes you and fades away. I tell myself there will be nothing afterwards. But I don't understand what it means. Sometimes I almost can . . . and then it fades away and I start thinking about the pains again, bullets, explosions. I'm a materialist, I swear it to you; I'm not going crazy. But something's the matter. I see my corpse; that's not hard but I'm the one who sees it, with my eyes. I've got to think . . . think that I won't see anything anymore and the world will go on for the others. We aren't made to think that." (Sartre, 1948, in Kaufmann, 1956, p. 231)

AUTHENTICITY, DESPAIR, AND MEANING

Even though this sense of anguish can be, to say the least, overwhelming, existentialists stress that to be open to these experiences is the one task which must be accomplished by "authentic" individuals. They stress, as Kierkegaard does (1944), that to learn *rightly* about being anxious is the most important lesson to be learned by human beings, being able to inform their lives by looking death "in the eyes."

It seems, however, that at the present time, a large section of the population suffers *wrongly* from this "existential despair," attempting to deny or "coverup" the reality of change and death. This is not to say that most of the American population has a dark and bleak view of life. Indeed, a recent national survey indicated that 41 percent of the U.S. working population is basically "upbeat" about people in general and about their work (Kanter & Mirvis, 1989). However, "feeling upbeat" can itself be a cover-up of a deeper sense of despair, as we will see later. In this sense, while the work force is often only described as more demanding, aggressive, educated, wishing to establish a professional status and expertise or realizing their ambition, a great deal of evidence seems to indicate that, for many, the "soul has gone stale." I will first mention some of these signs in society in general before speaking about organizations.

Signs of "existential despair," or to put it differently, the fact that some individuals are increasingly focusing on their "self" in society in general as an attempt to escape this despair, are numerous. For example, when asked if they would like to change something about their physical appearance, 96 percent of Americans answered positively, leading the researchers to state that "a solid majority of the American people are close to being 'obsessed' with their physical appearance" (Harris, 1987, p. 3).

As another, and more dramatic, sign of this despair, suicides of young U.S. men (14 to 25 years of age) have increased by 243 percent from 1960 to 1985, while this number has increased by 280 percent in Canada and 242 percent in France (U.S. Bureau of Census, 1990). Currently, for all age categories, it is estimated that suicide attempts have doubled or tripled in most industrial countries in the past 20 years (OMS, 1985).

In another domain, cocaine, an "existential" drug par excellence, giving a sensation of well-being, omnipotence, and an illusive feeling of "being truly alive," had been found to be the drug rising the fastest in popularity. In the 1980s, it was estimated that 1 out of 9 teenagers used his drug on a regular basis (Harris, 1987, P. 75), this trend subsequently having been accentuated with the introduction of "crack."

As another example, the development of a number of new sports, focusing on brief but exhilarating moments and providing an enhanced sense of "being alive," is troubling: In France, these new sports include "white water rafting," the "windspeed," the "deltaplane," or the "hydrospeed" (Dussard, 1988). In Brazil, the new "challenge" for some is "rail surfing," attempting to stay upright atop a moving train. In 1987, 150 "rail surfers" were killed in Rio, and 400 others were injured (Maier, 1988).

Such symptomatic despair is also reflected in the increased violence present in society. For example, in New York, 23 percent of young blacks 20 to 29 years of age were (as of 1989) either in jail or on probation (Fontaine, 1990). As a last evidence, a great number of therapists and other mental health professionals have stressed that their patients are no longer complaining of "classical neuroses," as described by Freud, such as fixations or phobias. Rather, these patients are now more likely to complain of a "diffuse dissatisfaction with life" or the experience of futility, boredom, and anxiety (Cooper, 1986; Kohut, 1971, 1984; Laing, 1961; Lasch, 1978; Menaker, in Detrick & Detrick, 1989; Rogers, 1980; Saint-Laurent, 1987).

Echoing the present "despair" in society at large, a large number of studies indicate that this trend is present in organizations as well. While these signs are diverse, they nonetheless suggest that the activity of work itself today is providing little meaning for employees. For example, a recent major national survey of the American work force has indicated that extrinsic rewards such as salary, benefits, and security are as important or more important than the employees' satisfaction with work itself (Schiemann & Morgan, 1983). As another sign, after interviewing personally more than 4,000 male senior executives, managers, and professionals in Fortune 500 companies, a researcher concluded that "men are disillusioned by the fruits of their success, for it has often resulted in emptiness and confusion" (Halper, 1988, p. 9). As still an additional indication, in another national survey, researchers found that 55 percent of the American work force believe that the average person is "not concerned with others' problems," stressing that "selfishness is a fundamental component of human character" (Kanter & Mirvis, 1989).

Increasingly experiencing a deep lack of personal and organizational meaning, it seems that a large segment of the work force, including top executives and workers, are currently using a number of perverse means in an attempt to escape or coverup these existential issues. For example—and echoing the increased use of drugs in society in general—executive drug abuse has increased dramatically. In a cover story in *Fortune*, a medical director operating 160 hospitals declared that he has seen a 100 percent increase in the number of high-level executives coming for treatment as compared with five years earlier, stating that "drugs have taken the business world by storm" (Flax, 1987). It should be stressed that addiction does not involve only the use of drugs, but is also seen in organizations as addiction to alcohol, work, destructive relationships, "winning," dramatic behaviors, overcommitment, or abrasive competition (Schaef & Fassel, 1988; Aubert and de Gaulejac, 1991).

In the same vein, a *Business Week* cover story, entitled "Fast-track Kids," described the characteristics of "hot" MBAs entering major U.S. corporations. While the author characterizes these individuals as "better educated, more self-confident and less fearful," she also stresses the darker side of these "rising stars." She stated that they exhibit some of the strongest characteristics of grandiose and omnipotent behaviors, such as the inability to delay gratification and lack of empathy:

> They are impatient for raw management authority, they develop little loyalty to the institutions they work for, and they're often charged with lacking the sensitivity and people skills that typify today's most suc-

cessful executives. These traits could also result in dramatic cultural changes in big corporations as the fast-track kids become the chief executives of the 21st century. (Davis, 1986)

To acknowledge the existence of "existential despair" and the attempt of some individuals to overcompensate for it through dramatic behaviors allows us to understand more fully the current idealization of grandiose and flamboyant leaders, as described, for example, by Reich (1987). As a sign of this idealization, the autobiographies of organizational leaders such as Iacocca, Goldsmith, or Trump all have had a place on the *New York Times* best-seller list. Perhaps it is Wansell, Goldsmith's biographer, who best expressed this idealization by Americans of these grandiose leaders when he wrote that "(Goldsmith) . . . lives out the fantasies of others with a flamboyance that is unmistakable" (Wansell, 1987, p. 11). However, while this type of leadership can diminish the existential despair of leaders themselves, providing them with a sense of perfection mirrored by an audience, and as well can diminish the followers' sense of despair through their idealization of their leader (Pauchant 1991), this type of leadership is often detrimental for the individuals involved, organizations, and society as a whole. As stressed by Bennis:

> In today's adoration not of the magi but of the CEOs, the public seems not to care that it is being damned, that not only the T. Boone Pickenses and the Carl Icahns but even the Lee Iacoccas are building their individual power bases at the expenses of the greater community. (Bennis, 1989, p. 74)

It is not easy to identify precisely the major underlying factors motivating this feeling of "existential despair" and its dangerous overcompensation. A large number of authors from various fields have pointed to a variety of factors such as the decline of the family, community, civic and religious heritage (Bellah, Madsen, Sullivan, Swider, & Tipton, 1985); the decrease of parental empathy or guidance (Kohut, 1984; Lasch, 1979); the perverse effect of the "scientific management" paradigm leading to a dehumanization of work and disillusion (Aktouf, 1986; Chanlat & Dufour, 1985); the false expectations set up by the new age movement (Bennis, 1989; Yankelovich, 1981); the too-great importance given to the standard economic criteria in organizational life and the lack of ethics (Mitchell & Scott, 1990; Pauchant & Fortier, 1990); the desacralization of society and its lack of spirituality (Grof & Grof, 1990; Peck, 1978); the increase of global turbulence, chaos, complexity, competition, economic uncertainty, and crises (Ackoff, 1981; Emery & Trist,

1973; Mitroff & Pauchant, 1990; Pauchant & Mitroff, 1992); the current focus on "utilitarian individualism," "narcissism" and "heroship" (Auber & Pages, 1989; Bellah et al., 1985; Enriquez, 1989; Lasch, 1979); the lack of "substantive" leadership (Bennis, 1989; Zaleznik, 1989); and many more factors.

Whatever the reasons for this existential despair and its overcompensating counterpart, many authors have commented on its disastrous effects on individuals, organizations, society in general, and the environment. In a recent article reviewing the abundant and heterogeneous literature on this subject, two organizational scientists have concluded that

> the evidence is massive that we, as a society, are degrading our physical environment, have a significant portion of our population that is alienated from the rest of society and have engaged in widely reported amounts of fraud, crime, and unethical behavior. (Mitchell & Scott, 1990, p. 25)

CURRENT ATTEMPTS TO DIMINISH EXISTENTIAL DESPAIR IN ORGANIZATIONS

In a recent book, Zaleznik has argued that management theory and practice was currently overconcerned with "process" to the detriment of "substance" (Zaleznik, 1989). Considering the extent of the experience of "existential despair," it is not surprising that the practice of management, as well as our theories and research in the domain, are more targeted toward an *attempt at diminishing this sense of despair* as opposed to focusing on the more substantive issues of business per se (Mitroff & Pauchant, 1990). This overconcern about the "process" of business is visible in the increase of new fashionable trends in management theory and practice, including "symbolic management," "strategic visioning," "corporate identity," "marketing of self," "total quality," "image management," "paper entrepreneurship," "interpretative strategies," and "cultural management," among others.

Perhaps one of the strongest signs of the importance of these new trends has been proposed by a recent analysis of corporate philosophy statements (Pearce & Davis, 1987). This study has revealed that contemporary organizations shy away from the more traditional and substantial definitions of business based on product and services, markets, or "core technology" (Thompson, 1967). Rather, it seems that nowadays organizations place the realization of their existential concerns as their fundamental purpose for conducting business. Reviewing the philosophic statements of 61 *Fortune* 500 companies, these researchers have found that the four most mentioned categories in these statements, were, in decreasing order: (a) *Concerns for survival* (expressed in 90 percent of the reviewed philosophical statements), (b) *Desired public image* (87%); (c) *Basic beliefs and philosophy* (79%); and (d) *Company self-concept* (77%). These concerns have to be compared with four more "traditional" areas of business such as: (e) *Commitment to principal products and services* (67%), (f) *Intended targeted customers and markets* (48%); (g) *Intended geographic areas of business* (41%), and (i) *Definition of core technology* (20%).

REEXAMINING THE "SEARCH FOR EXCELLENCE"

While the different trends so far mentioned stress the importance of existential issues in corporations, it seems that a single theme—the "search for excellence"—captures, perhaps better than all the others, the essence of what could be called the *search for existence.* Literally, this trend has taken by storm corporate America and organizations in other parts of the world. Peters and Waterman have sold more than 5 million copies of *In Search of Excellence*, this book having been translated in 15 languages. Tom Peters' subsequent books (Peters & Austin, 1985; Peters, 1988) also remained on the *New York Times'* best seller list for long periods. Indeed, the "search for excellence" had become the buzz-word for the 1980s, with numerous corporations, universities, governmental agencies, or other organizations stating it as their company self-concept and philosophy, and as their strategic means for "surviving" and competing successfully.

To understand how this trend is an expression of the existential tradition, the book *In Search of Excellence* needs to be given a more careful reading. At a more superficial level, it appears that Peters and Waterman have defined an "excellent" company through the use of financial criteria, claiming that they have chosen these companies as being "in the top half of (their) industry" for a continual period of 20 years, and on at least 4 of the 6 following criteria of "long-term superiority" (Peters & Waterman, 1982, pp. 22–23): Asset growth, equity growth, ratio of market value to book value, and returns on total capital, equity, and sales.

In addition, these authors stress that they have refined their analysis by measuring the degree of innovation of the chosen companies, based on the rating of industry experts. After having presented these criteria of "superiority," Peters and Waterman describe their famous eight criteria that, they claim, all excellent companies have implemented.

It is very interesting to note that most of the commentaries and criticisms offered on Peters and Waterman's arguments have only addressed these financial ratios or these eight criteria, thus missing the deeper message offered by the book. For example, some have argued that the "excellent companies" chosen by Peters and Waterman were not as financially superior as shown in the study, or others have stressed that some of the "criteria for excellence" posed a number of problems (Hoffman, 1986).

A more careful reading of the Peters and Waterman's argument shows, however, that they have attempted to answer the "existential despair" addressed by existentialists. Indeed, these authors, in the sixth page of their introduction, posit that the "magic" of excellent companies resides in the theory advanced by *Ernest Becker*, one of the most influential of the existential writers, who won the Pulitzer Prize in 1973 for his book *The Denial of Death*. As stated by Peters and Waterman:

> Discussions of management psychology have long focused on theory X or theory Y, the value of job enrichment, and, now, quality circles. They don't go far toward explaining the magic of the turned-on work force in Japan or in the American excellent company, but useful theory does exist. The psychologist Ernest Becker, for example, has stated a major supporting theoretical position, albeit one ignored by most management analysts. . . . About the winning team, Becker notes: "Society . . . is a vehicle for earthly heroism. . . . Man transcends death by finding meaning for his life . . . It is the burning desire for the creature to count. . . . What man really fears is not so much extinction, but extinction with insignificance. (Peters and Waterman, 1982, pp. xxii-xxiii)

Indeed, this statement indicates the inherent paradox existing in Peters and Waterman's book. On the first hand, they claim that they have identified "excellent" companies through the use of "objective" financial criteria, as stressed by classical economic and finance theories; and, on the other, they posit that excellent companies are the ones that have finally addressed the threat of "extinction by insignificance," as stressed by the existential tradition. However, it seems clear that Peters and Waterman *considered the existential position as the psychological bedrock of corporate "excellence."* Again, as they have stated, toward the end of *In Search of Excellence*:

The skill with which the excellent companies develop their people recalls that grim conflict . . . our basic need for security versus the need to stick out, the "essential tension" that the psychoanalyst Ernest Becker described. . . . (Peters & Waterman, 1982, p. 323)

It seems that the tremendous success of the "search for excellence" in corporations has been strongly motivated by this search for existential meaning by managers, striving to find an "overall" and "practical" solution to the problem of death. Unfortunately, while Peters and Waterman claim that they have based their principles on Ernest Becker's work, they have however only partially presented his argument, shying away from Becker's in-depth analysis of the inescapable issue of death. While a rigorous comparison of Becker's work with the arguments developed in *In Search of Excellence* still remains to be developed, I have noted below some of the most obvious contradictions.

Peters and Waterman propose that the search for "heroship," both at the individual and organizational levels, "transcends" existential despair. Quoting parts of Becker's work, they propose that individuals will be willing to commit or "surrender" themselves to the purpose of an organization if this organizational purpose provides them with a sense of greater meaning, and at the same time, they will wish to "stand out" by themselves in these organizations, striving to accomplish their own ambition. As stated by these authors:

Men willingly shackle themselves to nine-to-five if only the cause is perceived to be in some sense great. The company can actually provide the same resonance as does the exclusive club or honorary society. At the same time, however, each of us needs to stick out—even, or maybe particularly, in the winning institutions. So we observed, time and again, extraordinary energy exerted above and beyond the call of duty when the worker . . . is given even a modicum of apparent control over his or her own destiny. (Peters & Waterman, 1982, p. xxiii)

While it is true that Becker spoke of the quasi-necessity for human beings to engage in "earthy heroism," that is, heriosm springing from the culture in which individuals are immersed, and "personal heroism," that is, a creative act separated out of the common pool of shared meanings, he spoke of these heroisms as an *escape* from human "authenticity." As a true existentialist, Becker situated the human condition squarely within the context of the struggle with the issue of death. For him the realization that it takes 60 years or so of tremendous effort to make an individual and then that this individual is "only good for dying," is the basic paradox to be dealt with (Becker, 1973, p. 69). Arguing that society is a symbolic action system serving as a vehicle for earthy heroism for the purpose of denying the inescability of death, he stressed that the task of "authentic" individuals is to challenge the sources and the validity of these heroisms and to realize their dangerous illusions. As he stated:

> Human heroics is a blind driveness that burns people up; in passionate people, a screaming for glory as uncritical and reflexive as the howling of a dog. In the more passive of mediocre men it is disguised as they humbly and complainingly follow out the roles that society provides for their heroics and try to earn their promotions within the system. (Becker, 1973, p. 6)

Thus, while for Becker, "heroism" is indeed the most common response for human beings to the issue of death, as argued by Peters and Waterman, this type of heroism also leads for Becker to a denial of an "authentic" human condition, through the denial of death.

This difference between Peters and Waterman's argument and Becker's is also apparent in the claim made in *In Search of Excellence* that "excellent" companies allow their employees to become "heroes" and "give people control over their destinies." In the same vein, these authors stressed that organizations could make "meaning for people," turning "the average Joe and the average Jane into winners" (Peters & Waterman, 1982. p. 239).

Becker's own argument is different. Throughout his work, he argues that the search for and discovery of meaning is a *personal* experience, individuals having to feel and to believe by *themselves* that what they are doing is "truly heroic, timeless and supremely meaningful" (Becker, 1978, p. 6). In a long discussion, he describes "unauthentic" individuals, who "do not belong to themselves, are not 'their own persons,' do not act from their own center, do not see reality on its terms" (p. 73). In the same section, he gives examples of unauthentic individuals who did not create meaning from themselves, such as "the corporation men in the West or the bureaucrat in the East." Further, he describes a continuum of "unauthenticity," starting at one extreme from the "depressive psychosis," that is, individuals who are afraid of being themselves and fearful of exerting their individuality, and, at the other extreme, "schizophrenic psychosis" where individuals experience a sense of inflation of inner fantasy and symbolic possibility (Becker, 1973, pp. 77–79).

Thus, far from advocating that the "resolution" of the existential despair of death is for an individual "to be made heroic" by society or an organization, Becker stressed that "healthy," "true," "real" individuals are the ones who have transcended themselves by realizing the "truth" of their situation, by dispelling the lies of their characters and of their cultural heritage, by realizing their own mortality (p. 86).

Similarly, it also seems that Peters and Waterman have too quickly operationalized their version of Becker's work by stressing the paramount importance of ceremonies and rituals for developing this sense of "heroship." As they stated:

> Ritual is the technique for giving life. [Man's] sense of self worth is constituted symbolically, his cherished narcissism feeds on symbols, on an abstract idea of his own worth. Man's natural yearning can be fed limitlessly in the domain of symbols. (Peters & Waterman, 1982, p. xxiii)

As an example of this "symbolic management," much in vogue today in organizations, Peters and Waterman have pointed to a team of IBM's salesmen being applauded by executives, colleagues, family members, and friends while emerging from the player's tunnel of a stadium. Contrary to this view, Becker warned of the dangers of building a "compulsive character," building extra-thick defenses against existential despair and anxiety. Quoting Kierkegaard and echoing Sartre's concept of "bad faith," he stressed that "for a partisan of this most rigid orthodoxy, truth is an ensemble of ceremonies" (p. 71). Rather, as seen previously, Becker urged human beings to question the artifacts by which they live their lives and to derive by themselves their sense of meaning.

Finally, it seems that the overall purposes of Peters and Waterman and of Becker were fundamentally different. While Peters and Waterman were concerned with increasing organizational efficiency, productivity, and competitiveness, Becker explored the denial of death by human beings, including compulsive drives toward efficiency, productivity, and competitiveness. As such, Becker warned his readers not to surrender themselves to pseudo-"heroics," moving from one role or task to the other, deriving from them the illusion of controlling one's life. This contrasts sharply with the following comments made by Peters and Waterman, stressing the utilitarian purpose of "heroism," with the danger of becoming a means for management to control their employees by giving them an illusion of control:

In a field called "illusion of control" . . . findings indicate that if people think they have even modest personal control over their destinies, they will persist at tasks. They will do better at them. They will become more committed to them. (Peters & Waterman, 1982, p. 80)

To conclude this short discussion of the use of Becker's work by Peters and Waterman, it seems apparent that these authors have only taken on a part of this work—missing key elements. On the positive side, it is clear that Peters and Waterman have touched on the problem of existential despair and have attempted to provide some resolutions to this anguishing issue. As human beings we must empathize with their efforts to tackle such a crucial problem. I see this contribution as perhaps the most important reason why the trend toward "excellence" is so popular in organizations, beyond the issues of corporate survival, innovation, or competition: Indeed, the "search for excellence" appears to be a viable solution to appeasing the "staleness of our souls." However, when taking the totality of Becker's argument, it seems that the "solutions" proposed by Peters and Waterman lead in fact to *more* despair, pushing people and organizations alike in a vicious circle of "bad faith," as we will see later. Further, the "search for excellence" runs the potential danger of being absorbed by top executives, sustaining, through symbolic management, an illusion of heroship for their employees in quest of utilitarian purposes. On this note, it is unfortunate that Peters and Waterman did not emphasize the potential dangers inherent in the "search for excellence." For example, they acknowledge only briefly that there exists a "potential dark side" in this search for excellence, managers being tempted to "do almost anything" to accomplish this search (Peters & Waterman, 1982, p. 59), or that the "search for excellence" could lead in some instances to a "search for arrogance" (Peters, 1986).

Paradoxically, while Peters and Waterman have only taken from Becker's work what they needed to make their argument, the success of *In Search of Excellence* pays an indirect tribute to the value of Becker's work. To some extent, the success of this book is a vivid demonstration of the exactitude of Becker's argument, that is, that individuals and organizations can precipitate themselves with great energy into all sorts of realities for denying the inescability of death and for hiding themselves in the illusion of heroship. As stated by Becker:

The defenses that form a person's character support a grand illusion, and when we grasp this we can understand the full driveness of man.

He is driven away form himself, from self-knowledge, self-reflection.
. . . Anxiety lures us on . . . we flirt with our own growth, but also
dishonestly. . . . We seek stress, we push our own limits, but we do it
with our screen against despair. . . . We do it with the stock market,
with sports cars, with atomic missiles, with the success ladder in the
corporation or the competition in the university. (Becker, 1973 p. 56)

The problems surrounding Peters and Waterman's use of Becker's
work would not be such an issue if the trend in the "search for
excellence," as currently applied by many organizations, had not
had such a devastating effect on the individuals and organizations
involved. Already, a number of independent researchers, from Europe and North America, have argued that this trend has amplified
the "existential despair" experienced by some employees, the "depressive psychosis" pointed to by Becker, as well as increased the
dangers of the overcompensating behaviors that this despair triggers, as expressed by aspects of schizophrenic psychosis.

For example, Enriquez (1989) has argued that "excellent" companies lead their employees to become their "prisoners", with individuals losing their own "body, thinking and psyche". This author
stresses that these companies have a destructive effect on society as
a whole, focusing on short-term gains, financial manipulations, and
symbolic management. In a study conducted in one of the most
famous "excellent companies," Pagés, Bonetti, de Gauleac, & Descendre (1979) have shown how this company has become a "religious system," incarnating the wish for immortality. In other studies, Aubert and Pagés (1989) and Aubert and de Gaulejac (1991)
have documented the tremendous stress and despair experienced by
these employees, requiring them to become constant "warriors" and
"winners."

In North America, Kanter and Mirvis (1989) have proposed that
the promises made by the trend for "excellence" have increased
cynicism to an even greater extent in the employees, setting up
expectations that cannot be fulfilled. Miller (1990) has shown that
"exceptional" companies can bring about their own downfall, calling
it the "Icarus paradox." Schwartz (1987) has argued that the search
for "excellence" can lead to "organizational totalitarianism," defining "happiness" for their employees. In our own research, we have
found that strong beliefs in "excellence" contribute to the occur-
rence of major industrial disasters, managers denying the need for a
serious engagement in crisis management (Pauchant, 1988; Mitroff
& Pauchant, 1990; Pauchant & Mitroff, 1992).

It seems rather easy to criticize Peters and Waterman's call for an
organizational "excellence" as a way to decrease its employees' exis-

tential despair and to increase the firm's competitiveness and efficiency in a global economy. This dream is not new. As early as 1897,
the French sociologist Emile Durkheim believed that only the professional organization (as opposed to the church, the state, the community, or the family) could provide a solution to the anemic experience of individuals in a modern society and to the problem of suicide
(Durkheim, 1976). However, one can challenge the validity of this
dream, considering the economic and political realities of organizations. Further, to criticize the "search for excellence," in organizations or in other places, also goes against one of the most fundamental human wishes to decrease feelings of despair. To some extent,
and as Becker reminds us, many of us are "addicted to heroism,"
going from heroic to heroic in an attempt "to feel alive," not having
the courage to face the "total" and "multifaceted" reality of life and
death. The urging by existentialists to "face" life with all its poten-
tiality and pain, but without the support of illusive heroics, could be
indeed terrifying and requires courage and maturity. . . . It is, indeed, the *authentic* "hero's journey," described in mythology, with
all its terrors and marvels (Campbell, 1949). As warned by Becker,
most "people have psychotic breaks when repression no longer
works, when the forward momentum of activities is not longer possible" (Becker, 1973, p. 23). And yet, considering the extent of
environmental pollution, "societal pollution," and "soul pollution"
or considering the impact of major industrial disasters associated
with this "search for excellence," this urging becomes paramount,
in practice as well as in concept.

THE POTENTIAL CONTRIBUTION OF THE EXISTENTIAL TRADITION TO MANAGEMENT AND ORGANIZATION CHANGE

Considering the challenge that the existential tradition brings to
traditional and "excellent" management, it is not surprising that, so
far, only a handful of management scholars have made explicit use
of this tradition in their work.

Reviewing this literature at the end of the 1980s, Burrell and
Morgan (1979) had difficulties in finding examples of studies using
a "radical humanist approach," as they called it, in management.
While they mentioned a dozen authors of "general works," they only
referred to three studies in the field of management per se, although
they drew more from the works of Marx and Habermas than from the
existential tradition itself (Burrell & Morgan, 1979, pp. 320-

321). As they stated at that time, these studies could "best be understood as attempts to articulate elements of the radical humanist approach to the study of organizations" (Burrell & Morgan, 1979, p. 319). About five years later, Morgan (1986) again reviewed this literature and mentioned only three of the studies mentioned below.

Since then, a greater—but still lilliputian—number of authors have produced works in the field of management, grounding their analysis in the existential tradition itself, or borrowing from it, in addition to other perspectives. For example, Aktouf (1990) has documented in a case study the existence of a different and more "enlightened" kind of leadership in an organization, inspired by Shakespeare's King Lear's dilemma. Boland and Hoffman (1983) showed how employees in a machine shop used humor as a way to preserve their existential meaning. Similarly, Bouchard (in Chanlat, 1990, pp. 589–611) proposed that the expression of symbolism in organizations springs from an existential wish to create. Denhardt (1987) argued that the superior-subordinate relationship was based on the imagery of the master-slave relationship as a quest for immortality, while in a book (Denhardt, 1981), he explored the way in which the world of organizations affects its employees' sense of meaning, action, and sense of continuity. Also in a book, Guillet de Monthoux (1983) challenged the traditional views of decision-making and bureaucracy theory through anarchism and existential philosophies. Morgan (1986, pp. 212–214), reviewing briefly Becker's work, has noted that this perspective suggests that much behavior within organizations can be explained in terms of a quest for immorality.

In another book, Pagés (1984) proposed, using the notion of "mitsein" developed by Heidegger, that the affective reality of a group or an organization does not emerge primarily from each of its members, but rather obeys first a group logic. Schwartz, in a series of articles, discussed (1985) the implications of the denial of death on organizational change efforts, while he argued (1987a) that antisocial actions of organizationally committed individuals are motivated by a quest for self-identity and meaning. He also proposed (1987b) that the idea of a perfect organization leads to totalitarianism with disastrous effects such as slavishness, shamefulness, cynicism, loneliness, and alienation. In a recent book, Schwartz (1990) also applied the model of Alcoholics Anonymous to organizational theory and practice.

In yet another series of articles, Sievers (1986a, 1986b) argued that a number of concepts in management, such as participation or motivation, are "scientific inventions," being taken as surrogates for existential meaning, and he proposed (1987) that the rejection of death in organization theory and practice is obsolete, death having to be seen as part of the normal course of life.

Finally, in two books, we described 24 "dangerous games," that is, games leading to organizational disasters, that are presently played in organizations in an attempt to diminish the symbolic sense of death of organizational members themselves (Mitroff & Pauchant, 1990), and we discussed some of the implications of existential issues in crisis management, developing the concept of "bounded emotionality" (Pauchant and Mitroff, 1992).

While these studies have been produced by management scientists, we can also mention here a number of works written by existentialists themselves addressing the field of management. In particular, Maslow's book *Eupsychian Management* (1965) can be considered a classic on the subject. While Maslow is not often seen a such, he must be considered as strongly existentialist, as he was keenly interested in the problem of "evasion from growth" and the "fear of standing alone," calling it the "Jonah Syndrome" (see Becker, 1973, pp. 47–52).

In addition, a number of existential works, although fictional, could be used in management education for discussing existential issues in the field, such as dramatic and destructive leadership: *Moby Dick* (Melville) or *MacBeth* (Shakespeare); alienation from work and self-estrangement: *Death of a Salesman* (Miller) or *The Metamorphises* (Kafka); the existential effect of bureaucracies: *1984* (Orwell) or *The Castle* (Kafka); organizational conflicts and coalitions: *The Brothers Karamozov* (Dostoevsky) or *Animal Farm* (Orwell); and many others. Indeed these fictional works are such rich sources for capturing existential issues in management that we see the use of this literature as one of the fundamental contributions of the existential tradition to management, in addition to the fields of existential philosophy and existential psychology.

TOWARD A FIELD OF ORGANIZATIONAL EXISTENTIALISM

The need persists to establish in the study of management and organization change a field of "organizational existentialism" and to legitimize the use, research, and publication of such a perspective in the future. At this time, it is difficult to predict what will be the outcomes of such a field of theory and practice. One may, however consider four general potential outcomes.

First, it is likely that such a perspective will offer a radically different view of organizing and of its purpose. This contribution seems particularly important at a time when a number of management scholars have critiqued the rigidity of our field and its increasing lack of relevance for managers (Cummings, 1983; Daft & Lewin, 1990; Luthans, 1986).

Second, the use of this tradition will force researchers to collect grounded, concrete, personal, subjective, and phenomenological data, drawing from the "radical humanist" research perspective (Burrell & Morgan, 1979), or the "particular humanist" scientific paradigm (Mitroff & Kilmann, 1982). Such an inquiry will thus contribute to reintroducing the person as "subject" (rather than "object") in the organizational sciences, and in organizations themselves (Chanlat, 1990).

Third, such an inquiry could increase the amount of empathy toward organizational members, especially when confronted with changes that challenge fundamentally their personal meaning and sense of self. Taking the search for existential meaning *seriously*, an existential view of work could thus lead to more humanistic view of organizing and of the process of change (Tannenbaum & Hanna, 1985; Schein, 1990).

And fourth, while the existential tradition has been criticized as being "hominocentric," that is, making the person as "everything," and as being "immature," that is, focusing on problems of self-identity (for an example of such criticisms, see Kaplan, 1961, pp. 97–128), the struggle of individuals with existential issues could also be seen as a *necessary stage of development* toward a different maturity and wisdomm, grounded in the transpersonal realm. As argued by Kierkegaard (1944) or Rank (1961), for example, the existential tradition can thus also be seen as a step toward another realm of experience—as a necessary stage toward spirituality, with a number of challenging avenues for management. In this sense, the search for existential "authenticity," rather than "excellence," can be regarded as a distinctive stage of development, extending to an additional and complementary level of consciousness in human systems.

REFERENCES

Ackoff, R. L. (1981). *Creating the corporate future. Plan or be planned for.* New York: John Wiley and Sons.

Aktouf, O. (1986). *Le travail industriel contre l'homme?* Alger: ENAL/OPU.

Aktouf, O. (1990). Immortality, managerial taboos and leadership. A theoretical framework and a case study. Working paper, HEC, University of Montreal, Montreal, Canada.

Aubert, N. & V. de Gaulejac (1991). Le coût de l'excellence. Paris: Seuil.

Aubert, N., & M. Pagés (1989). *Le stress professionel*. Paris: Klincksieck.

Becker, E. (1973). *The denial of death*. New York: The Free Press.

Bellah, R. N. R., Madsen, R., Sullivan, W. M., Swidler, A., & Tipton, S. M. (1985). *Habits of the heart. Indvidualism and commitment in American life*. Berkeley, CA: University of California Press.

Bennis, W. G. (1989). *Why leaders can't lead. The unconscious conspiracy continues*. San Francisco, CA.: Jossey Bass Publishers.

Boland, R. J., & Hoffman R. (1983). Humor in a machine shop. In L. Pondy, P. Frost, G. Morgan, & T. Dandridge (Eds.), *Organizational symbolism* (pp. 187–198). Greenwich, CT: JAI Press.

Buber, M. (1958). *I and thou* (2nd ed., transl. by R. G. Smith). New York: Charles Scribner's Sons.

Bugental, J. F. (1988). *The search for existential identity. Patient-therapist dialogues in humanistic psychotherapy*. San Francisco, CA.: Jossey-Bass.

Burrell, G., & Morgan, G. (1979). *Sociological paradigms and organizational analysis. Elements of the sociology of corporate life*. London-Exeter, New Hampshire: Heinemann.

Campbell, J. (1948). *The hero with a thousand faces*. Princeton, NJ: Princeton University Press.

Camus, A. (1951). *L'homme revolté*. Paris: Gallimard. (The rebel. An essay on man in revolt. New York: Vantage Books, 1956.)

Chanlat, A., & Dufour, M. (Eds.). (1985). *La rupture entre l'entreprise et les hommes. Le point de vue des sciences de la vie*. Montréal, Québec: Editions Québec/Amerique.

Chanlat, J-F. (Ed.). (1990). *L'individu dans l'organization. Les dimensions oubliées*. Québec: Presses de l'Université Laval/Paris: Eska.

Cooper, A. N. (1986). Narcissism. In A. P. Morrison (Ed.). *Essential papers on narcissim*. New York: New York University Press. (pp. 112–143)

Cummings, L. L. (1983). The logic of management. *Academy of Management Review 8*(4), 532–538.

Daft, R. L., & Lewin, A. Y. (1990). Can organization studies begin to break out of the normal science straitjacket? An editorial essay. *Organization Science, 1*(1), 1–9.

Davis, E. (1986, November 10). Fast-track kids. *Business Week*.

Denhardt, R. B. (1981). *In the shadow of organization*. Lawrence, KS: The Regent Press of Kansas.

Denhardt, R. B. (1987). Images of death and slavery in organizational life. *Journal of Management, 13*(3), 529–541.

De Tocqueville, A. (1956). *Democracy in America*. (Transl. by R. D. Heffner). New York: Mentor Books.

Detrick, D. W., & S. P. Detrick (1989) (Eds.). *Self psychology. Comparisons and contrasts*. Hillsdale, NJ: The Analytic Press.

Durkheim, E. (1976). *Le Suicide: Etude sociologique*. Paris: Presses Universitaires de France (Orig. published in 1897. Suicide. New York: Free Press, 1951).

Dussard, T. (1988, August 15). Nouveaux sports d'été: Comment se faire peur. *Le Point, 830*, 59–63.

Emery, F. E., & E. L. Trist (1973). *Toward a social ecology. Contextual appreciations of the future in the present*. London: Plenum Publishing Company.

Enriquez, E. (1989). L'individu pris au piege de la structure stratégique. *Connexions, 54*(2), 145–161.

Flax, S. (1987, June 24). The executive addict. *Fortune Magazine*, pp. 24–31.

Fontaine, A. (1990, October 26). Y a-t-il encore un "super grand"? *Le Monde*, Front page.

Friedman, M. (Ed.). (1964). *The worlds of existentialism. A critical reader*. New York: Random House.

Guillet de Monthoux, P. (1983). *Action and existence. Anarchism for business administration*. New York: John Wiley and Sons.

Grof, C., & Grof, S. (1990). *The stormy search of the self. A guide to personal growth through transformational crisis*. Los Angeles, CA: Jeremy P. Tarcher, Inc.

Halper, J. (1988). *Quiet desperation. The truth about successful men*. New York: Warner Books.

Harris, L. (1987). *Inside America*. New York: Vintage Books.

Heidegger, M. (1963). *Being and time* (Transl. by J. Macquarrie and E. Robison). New York: Harper and Row.

Hesse, H. (1963). *Steppenwolf* (Transl. by B. Creighton). New York: Bantam Books.

Hoeller, K. (Ed.). (1990). Readings in existential psychology and psychiatry. *Review of Existential Psychology and Psychiatry*, special issue, Vol. 20, Nos. 1, 2, and 3.

Hoffman, W. (1986). What is necessary for corporate moral excellence? *Journal of Business Ethics, 61*(5), 233–242.

Kafka, F. (1961). *Parables and paradoxes*. New York: Schocken Books.

Kanter, D. L., & P. H. Mirvis (1989). *The cynical Americans. Living and working in an age of discontent and disillusion*. San Francisco, CA.: Jossey-Bass.

Kaplan, A. (1961). *The new world of philosophy*. New York: Random House.

Kaufmann, W. (Ed.). (1956). *Existentialism. From Dostoevsky to Sartre*. New York: Meridian Books.

Kierkegaard, S. (1944). *The concept of dread* (Transl. by W. Lowrie). Princeton, NJ: Princeton University Press. (Original work published 1844)

Kohut, H. (1971). *The analysis of the self: A systematic approach to the psychoanalytic treatment of narcissistic disorders*. New York: International University Press.

Kohut, H. (1984). *How does analysis cure?* (ed. by A. Goldberg). Chicago: The University of Chicago Press.

Laing, R. D. (1961). *Self and others*. New York: Penguin Books.

Lasch, C. (1978). *The culture of narcissism. American life in the age of diminishing expectations.* New York: Warner books.

Luthans, F. (1986, August). *Fifty years later. What do we really know about managers and managing?* Presidential address, Academy of Management Meeting.

Maier, J. (1988, October 10). In Brazil: City surfing atop of wild trains. *Time Magazine.*

Maslow, A. (1965). *Eupsychian management. A journal.* Homewood, IL: Richard D. Irwin, Inc.

Maslow, A. (1971). *The farther reaches of human nature.* New York: Viking.

May, R. (1950). *The meaning of anxiety.* New York: Washington Square Press.

May, R., Angel, E., & Ellenberger, H. F. (Eds.). (1958). *Existence. A new dimension in psychiatry and psychology.* New York: Simon and Schuster.

McWhinney, W. (1980). Paedogenesis and other modes of design. In T. G. Cummings (Ed.), *System theory for organization development.* New York: Wiley.

McWhinney, W. (1992). Paths of change. Strategic choices for organizations and society. Newbury Park, CA.: Sage.

Miller, D. (1990). *The Icarus paradox. How exceptional companies bring about their own downfall.* New York: Haper Business.

Mitchell, T. R., & Scott, W. G. (1990). America's problems and needed reforms: Confronting the ethic of personal advantage. *Academy of Management Executive,* 4(3), 23–35.

Mitroff, I. I., & Kilmann, R. H. (1982). *Methodological approaches to social science.* San Francisco, CA: Jossey-Bass.

Mitroff, I. I., & Pauchant, T. C. (1990). *We're so big and powerful nothing bad can happen to us.* New York: Birch Lane Press.

Morgan, G. (1986). *Images of organization.* Beverly Hills, CA: Sage Publications.

Nietzsche, F. (1972). *Ainsi parlait Zarathoustra. Un livre pour tous et pour person.* Paris: Le Livre de Poche.

OMS (World Health Organization). (1985). *Les buts de la santé pour tous.* Copenhague.

Ortega y Gasset, J. (1958). *Man and crisis* (Transl. by M. Adams). New York: W. W. Norton.

Pagés, M., Bonetti, M., de Gauleac, V., & Descendre, D. (1979). *L'emprise de l'organisation.* Paris: Presses Unversitaires de France.

Páges, M. (1984). *La vie affective des groupes. Esquisse d'une théorie de la relation humaine.* (2nd. Ed.). Paris: Dunod.

Pauchant, T. C. (1988). *Crisis management and narcissism: A Kohutian perspective.* Unpublished dissertation. University of Southern California. Graduate School of Business Administration, Los Angeles, CA.

Pauchant, T. C. (1991). Transferential leadership. Towards a more complex understanding of charisma in organizations. *Organization Studies,* 12(4), 507–527.

Pauchant, T. C., & Fortier, I. (1990). Anthropocentric ethics in organiza tions. Strategic management and the environment: A typology. *Advances in Strategic Management, 6*, 99–114.

Pauchant, T. C., & Mitroff, I. I. (1988) Crisis prone versus crisis avoiding organizations. Is your organization culture your worst enemy in creating crises? *Industrial Crisis Quarterly, 2*(1), 53–63.

Pauchant, T. C., & Mitroff, I. I. (1992). *Transforming the crisis-prone organization. Preventing individual, organizational and environmental tragedies.* San Francisco: Jossey-Bass.

Pearce, J. A. III, & F. Davis (1987). Corporate mission and statements: The bottom line. *Academy of Management Executive, 1*(2), 109–116.

Peck, M. S. (1978). *The road less traveled. A new psychology of love, traditional values and spiritual growth.* New York: Simon and Schuster.

Peters, T. J., & Waterman, R. H., Jr. (1982). *In search of excellence. Lessons from America's best-run companies.* New York: Harper and Row.

Peters, T., & Austin, N. (1985). *A passion for excellence. The leadership difference.* New York: Random House.

Peters, T. (1986). In search of arrogance. In R. Nader & W. Taylor (Eds.), *The big boys. Power and position in American business* (pp. ix–xv). New York: Pantheon Books.

Peters, T. (1988). *Thriving on chaos. Handbook for a management revolution.* New York: Alfred A. Knopf.

Rank, O. (1961). *Psychology and the soul.* New York: Perpetua Books.

Reich, R. (1987, April 13). Tales of a new America. *Business Week*, pp. 16–18.

Rogers, C. (1980). *A way of being.* Boston: Houghton-Mifflin.

Saint-Laurent, C. (1987, August 3). Corps avez-vous donc une âme? *Le Point, 776*, 83–87.

Sartre, J-P. (1966). *Being and nothingness.* New York: Washington Square Press.

Schaef, A. W., & Fassel, D. (1988). *The addictive organization.* New York: Harper and Row.

Schein, E. H. (1990). Back is the future: Recapturing the O.D. vision. In F. Massarik (Ed.), *Advances in organization development* (Vol. 1, pp. 13–26). Norwood, NJ: Ablex.

Schwartz, H. (1985). The usefulness of myth and the myth of usefulness: A dilemma for the applied organization scientist. *Journal of Management, 11*(1), 31–42.

Schwartz, H. S. (1987a). Anti-social actions of commited organizational participants: An existential psychoanalytic perspective. *Organization Studies, 8*(4), 327–340.

Schwartz, H. S. (1987b). On the psychodynamics of organizations totalitarianism. *Journal of Management, 13*(1), 42–54.

Schwartz, H. S. (1990). *Narcissistic process and corporate decay: The theory of organization ideal.* New York: New York University Press.

Schiemann, W. A., & Morgan, B. S. (1983). *Managing human resources: Employee discontent and declining productivity.* Princeton, NJ: Opinion Research Corp.

Sievers, B. (1986a). Participation as a collusive quarrel over immortality. *Dragon 1*(1), 72–82.

Sievers, B. (1986b). Beyond the surrogate of motivation. *Organization Studies, 7*(4), 335–351.

Sievers, B. (1987). The diabolization of death. Some speculative thoughts on the obsolescence of mortality in organization theory and practice. In J. Hassard & D. Pym (Eds.), *Organizational inquiry: Critical issues in the theory of organizations* (pp. 50–72). London: Croom Helm.

Tannenbaum, R., & Hanna, B. W. (1985). Holding on, letting go and moving on: Understanding a neglected perspective on change. In R. Tannenbaum, N. Margulies, F. Massarik, & Associates (Eds.), *Human systems developmment. New perspective on people and organizations* (pp. 95–121). San Francisco, CA.: Jossey Bass.

Thompson, J. D. (1967). *Organizations in action.* New York: McGraw-Hill.

U.S. Bureau of the Census. (1990). *Statistical abstract of the United States: 1987* (110th ed.). Washington DC: Author.

Wansell, G. (1987). *Tycoon. The life of James Goldsmith.* New York: Atheneum.

Yankelovich, D. (1981). *New rules. Searching for self-fulfillment in a world turned upside down.* New York: Random House.

Zaleznik, A. (1989). *The managerial mystique. Restoring leadership in business.* New York: Harper and Row.

7

Networks as a Means of Organizational Development

Bernhard Vogt
University of Witten/Herdecke
Germany

Individuals and organizations find themselves in situations of increasing complexity and uncertainty. Furthermore, organization change manifests itself as a continuous need for organizations to cope with a "turbulent environment" that is highly dynamic (Borys & Jemison, 1987; Emery, 1982; Miles, 1989; Weisbord, 1987). We can observe dynamic changes in technical, social, economic, and—nowadays—even the political field.

In the technical field new systems of production technology—for instance, robots—are a challenge to organizations. Besides the possible "crowding out" of the human work force through automated machines, the information processing becomes a superior and pervasive value-creating activity for organizations. When information becomes an increasingly important factor, on one hand the proper technical handling and on the other hand the adopted mental processing assume strategic meaning. The ability to gather relevant information and to process it in the most appropriate way determines the strategic advantage of organizations.

As the world becomes a "global village" (McInnis, 1984), enhanced by the flow of information and capital and the mobility of human beings, new kinds of extensive tension can be identified in the world economy. This involves an internationalizing of products and services. Even cultural and societal values diffuse globally.

In the social field we can observe positive changes as people are relatively higher qualified at nearly all levels.[1] The economic force and technical equipment support decentralization of information processing and decision making. This is followed by higher responsibility of the future employee. It also increases the possibility for

---

[1] "Education is the thread that became dominant in the motive woven by the last phase of industrialism" (Emery, 1982, p. 1105).

employees to work more autonomously and to identify with their activity. As these developments open up the context of individuals, they can also become a danger to present social structures. As certain people are able to cope with turbulences and others are not, society may split into diverging groups. The gap between people developing themselves and others falling back to old norms can increase. In demographic terms, a relatively larger percentage of older people may also support this trend, unless counterbalanced by special efforts to facilitate revitalization, second and third careers and so on among the elderly.

Even in the political field we have observed tremendous changes. The dissolving of former political blocks in East and West, the unification of Germany, as well as increasing difficulties in many developing countries in South America, Africa, and Asia accelerate the pace of political reshaping.

These developments vary in different continents, countries, and cultural units. However, they represent general tendencies we ought to face. In many respects improvements have been realized. Still, a promising concept for understanding and designing these interdependencies is lacking. Particularly, the present industrial setting and its organization is connected to the changes mentioned above. Organizations are a crucial asset to maintaining economic performance. Furthermore, organizations offer a framework for human self-realization and the maintenance of social value systems

As this roughly describes the situation of society and the meaning of organization, we become aware that present modes of organization often seem inappropriate. Hierarchies with their formal regulations are overcharged when the environment is turbulent and complex. They become overloaded, their adaptation takes an increasing amount of time, and the quality of decision and action suffers (Willke, 1989). Thus, organizations try to cope with such a situation by accelerating their rhythms of adapting a formal setting. Others neglect these formal adaptations and foster improvisation. Both reactions seem to be reactive. However, it appears to be more appropriate to take exceptions and turbulences seriously by finding more suitable modes of organization in advance. Therefore, numerous authors now demand differentiation as a means to cope with increased complexity (Jarillo, 1988; Willke, 1989; Wimmer, 1989). One promising concept that is able to reflect on the interdependencies is the "network." Thinking in interdependencies and supporting this by changed physical settings seems to them facilitating— generating the necessary contingent complexity in organizations.

This chapter focuses on "networks," an emerging concept in organization theory. Even though networks have not been researched thoroughly, the concept has already affected practitioners. There is no single understanding of "networks"; rather, a variety of different interpretations exists. In this work, emphasis is placed on the meaning of networks and on their contribution for organization analyses and design. In addition I stress that structural reform is only a part of intended change. Moreover, I consider the cognitive adaption of a new paradigm as essential. That means that people have to develop new skills and perspectives towards organizations. Trying to improve the insights in network theory is not enough; operational follow-up in practice is called for.

I need to stress that the term networks that I use in the following discussion carries several meanings. The first meaning is *networks as organizational setting*. This mostly refers to a formal setting as opposed to markets and hierarchies (Ouchi, 1980). Secondly, networks are described as *system layers* which carry meaning and values for persons. These are productive, cultural, and personal networks (Johannisson, 1987b). In my opinion the concept of networks is a very adaptive and flexible means to view social reality.

The network concept offers a framework to view social settings and actions in more differentiated terms. It means that not only economic rationality in the form of instrumental structures determines social life, but that there also exists a value structure which is carried in communities as norms and on the individual level as affections. Based mainly on an exchange theory, the network concept unfolds at these different levels.

NETWORKS

Different Understandings

In the beginning networks occurred as a point of interest in different fields within the social sciences. Mainly, the concept was influenced by social anthropology, ethnology, sociology, and psychology. The orientation toward quantitative description of social interdependencies fostered concentration on mathematical graph theory and research of communication networks (Schenk, 1984). It can be assumed that these efforts were later followed by cybernetics and system theory starting to offer a framework for better insight in interdependent processes (Maturana, 1980; Luhmann, 1984). Later on this was followed by contingency theory, which tried to improve the understanding of the contingencies between situations or environment and actors, or more abstractly, between different system levels. Nowadays concepts of self-organization appear (Willke, 1989). These concepts supply a model according to which organizations can be seen as social systems. They are characterized, for example, by relative autonomy and self-reference (Ulrich and Probst, 1984). Chaos theories also now become interesting in regard to the understanding of social organisms. Networks also emerged as a form of organization within the framework of strategic management (Ouchi, 1980; Jarillo, 1988; Thorelli, 1986; Borys and Jemison, 1987).

In this tradition the network concept grew within the social sciences and also became part of the vocabulary in economics, business, and organization theory. Nevertheless, the positions still are very diverse, which becomes apparent by comparing the work of different authors.

Definition

Harris (1985, p. 249) offers an extensive and open definition of networks:

> Networking is another strategy of performance improvement that is prominent in the emerging work. It involves a system of interrelated people or groups, offices or work stations linked together for information, exchange and mutual support. This can be accomplished personally or electronically, informally and formally, locally and globally.

Thorelli (1986) described networks even more simply and generally: "A network may be generally described as a persisting identity of nodes and links."

At the same time Weick speaks of networks as "loosely coupled systems," he demands a more flexible understanding of networks. "There is danger of portraying organizations in inappropriate terms which suggest an excess of unity, integration, coordination and consensus." He argues "that elements may appear or disappear and may merge or become separated in response to need-deprivations within the individual, group and/or organization." (Weick, 1976, p. 5). Organizations seem to him much more determined by this functionality concerning their interdependence. Thus, it is logical for him that organizational settings will disappear or appear under certain conditions.[2]

---

[2] I would like to add that the process of creating new organizations is more likely to occur than abolishing old ones; for further discussion see Olson (1965) and Hedberg (1981).

Leveson (1986, p. 20) considers the emergence and need for networks:

> While networking has always been present, its use appears to be increasingly rapid and there is every indication that this trend will continue. It is becoming a central part of the structure of industry and the overall economy and is emerging as a dominant feature of the information age. Networking is having its greatest impact in the diverse international arena and the financial services industry, both of which are central to the evolution and the performance of the economy.

The observations of these various authors are mostly complementary. Their positions can be seen as multiple and in themselves establish cognitive networks.

Terminology

Two features are most important in describing and defining networks. These are *nodes* and *links*. These terms are generally recognized to reflect the basic structure of networks. Nodes represent the elements or units in the networks. Individuals, groups, departments, corporations, households, or associations can be nodes. Links are the connections between the nodes. They become established through the relations and interactions between the nodes, the elements of the network. The links are the essential medium for transactions. In human networks persons are nodes of networks as well as links.

Particularly, the scholar who is oriented towards "network analysis" as an analytical empirical tool needs to develop more formal frameworks. For Tichy (1981), two perspectives are very important for the network concept: (a) the "transactional content," and (b) the "network structure," (see Table 7.1).

The anthropologist Boissevain (1974) also contributed strongly to the network concept. Enhancing the contentional and structural description noted he distinguishes different network zones. He differentiates between first order, second order, third order to n-order zones (see Figure 7.1).

The single person, as the node in an ego network, and its ties to other nodes are considered the first-order zone. These nodes of the first-order zone itself consist of their own ego network. Mostly these nodes are not identical with the first ego network. However, the nodes of the second ego network can be viewed as nodes for the first one. Therefore, they are elements of a second-order zone. The network system itself can be redundant.

TABLE 7.1.   NETWORK PROPERTIES

Network properties	Explanations
Transactional content	The four media of exchange are: (a) expressions of affect, (b) influence, (c) information, and (d) goods and services.
Characteristics of links	
Reciprocity	To what degree are relationships symmetric rather than asymmetric or nonsymmetrical?
Clarity of norms	How clear are the ways participants should behave in relationships?
Intensity	To what degree will one participant disregard personal costs in order to fulfill obligations?
Multiplexity	In how many ways are one pair of participants related?
Structural characteristics	
Organizational density	What portion of the organizational members participate in this network?
Clustering	How many dense regions, such as coalitions or cliques, does this network contain?
Size	How many people participate in this network?
Visibility	Can uninvolved observers tell who participates in this network, and can participants themselves map their network?
Membership criteria	How clear are the criteria for recruitment or membership?
Openness	How many relationships does this network have with other networks? Are the participants cosmopolitans or locals?
Stability	How long is this network expected to survive?
Connectedness	Of all possible relationships among participants, what portion actually exist?
Reachability	What is the average number of links separating two participants?
Occupational density	What portion of all the occupations in the organization are included in this network?
Vertical density	What portion of all hierarchical levels does this network encompass?
Centrality	Does this network include many sociometric stars or only a few?
Key participants	
Star	A participant who has many relationships with other participants.
Liaison	A participant who links two or more clusters that would be separate otherwise.
Bridge or linking pin	A participant who belongs to multiple clusters.
Gatekeeper	A participant who controls the flow from one section of the network to another.
Isolate	A person who has no relationships to others.

FIGURE 7.1.   NETWORK ZONES

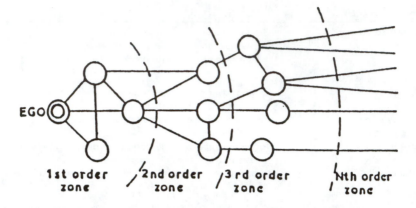

In addition, Boissevain (1974) distinguishes the interactions be-tween nodes. Transactions are unilateral and exchanges are bilat-eral interactions between nodes. Furthermore, process criteria are:

- diversity of linkages
- transactional content
- directional flow
- frequency and duration of interaction

and structural criteria are

- size
- density
- degree of connection
- clusters.

These criteria are similar to some in the table by Tichy and Fombrun (1979), and they supplement it in some parts.

NETWORKS AND ORGANIZATION DEVELOPMENT

Now, I would like to focus on the relevance of networks and partic-ularly network thinking for Organization Development (OD). First, I introduce a framework that gives some orientation to the basic structure on how networks can be viewed. This is followed by a description of a network concept that I view as helpful for discussion in OD. Finally there is a discussion on the concepts on organization development and its objectives.

The earlier understanding of organizations as bounded units in an environment that was considered as the restricting framework is to be rejected. This chapter sets out to focus on an emerging understanding of organization. Formerly, organization theory was affected by a strong need to view organizations as bounded. The theory assumed that there are limits for organizations that separate activities of different economic units. Without limits it seems to be impossible to order certain values to the performance of single organizational activities. Thus, limits indeed are an essential part of the market system to distribute rewards and sanctions.

Nevertheless, it becomes less and less clear what these limits look like, as the economic system is increasingly interconnected. Now it becomes obvious that individuals and organizations are much more interlocked with the environment than formerly taken into consideration. Earlier theoretical concepts on organization did not give much attention to the outer environment. Nowadays, induced through system theory, different system levels find more and more appreciation in theory. In practice we find corporations that lay claim to the responsibility for and active design of the environment.[3] They stress the function of corporations and associations placing themselves at the disposal as designers of culture and society[4], to counteract decline of cultural and societal conditions, not to mention the ecological threat.

Thus, the classical objectives of organization development with respect to "task accomplishment" and "human fulfillment" need to be expanded to take account of a positive "collective framework."[5] Table 6.2 provides a schematic survey:

---

[3] Even though it is an unsolved problem to differentiate individual, organizational, and social interests.

[4] See the proclamation of the Deutsche Bank AG, Mercedes Benz AG for a new "Ordnungspolitik."

[5] The level of society has to be considered as well. The strong need in society for ecological and social balance indicates a general development which is discussed nowadays. More concrete is the dependence of organizations on the institutional system, which became established collectively of a long tradition. We can even speak of a "printing" of society by institutional forms. It can be interpreted analogously to the socialization process of individuals. This affects not only the consumers' attitudes, but it also affects value systems and establishes traditional behavior. The changes of these settings is increasing. Therefore, it seems to be appropriate to introduce a level of objectives that refers to this social development (see also Olson, 1965). He maintains that the correlation of organizational interest in the setting of the environment increases with the size of the organization.

TABLE 7.2.

Perspectives	Network Layers	Objectives
Transaction costs	Production Network	Performance
Relationship	Personal Network	Individual Growth
Cultural Coherence	Cultural Network	Social Development

PERSPECTIVES

The Transaction Cost Theory is widely applied to networks (Ouchi, 1980; Borys, 1987). Williamson is the most prominent representative of the Transaction Cost Theory. It is a concept based on economic rationality giving information about the most efficient "governance structure." The alternatives to this theory are markets and hierarchies, as well as hybrid forms such as networks. This perspective is based on an instrumental commitment (Johannisson, 1987). The "backbone" of the Transaction Cost Theory is costs, which become viewed in a wider perspective. Attention is given to costs, which are connected with economic action, even though they do not exist in calculations of price determinations. However, the concept cannot cover the problems of imprecise or indefinite time horizons and incomplete knowledge about alternatives.[6] There is no ideal way of assigning costs to different actions.

The relationship perspective is primarily characterized by a social viewpoint. It emphasizes that a basic interest in exchange and communication exists among people. This is a force for individuals to establish relationships which occur spontaneously. A master plan does not exist about who is going to establish a relationship with whom. Even the choice of the "arena" where social interaction takes place often is not reflected.

Cultural coherence indicates that individuals develop in a certain cultural setting. This is often determined by the geographic arena in which people grow up. Besides this overlapping in the national or regional heritage, other values can affect it. While often not clearly conscious to the individual, such cultural coherence will always be a latent factor in life. We can observe that people who emigrated often

---

[6] For further critique see also Johanson and Mattson, 1987, p. 34.

still retain a certain identification and attachment to their country of origin, with regional and ethic factors interacting.

So, having described certain perspectives on which human interaction is based, we can now view the network level. I would like to point out that the perspectives and the networks are not directly associated with one another. There is an overlapping set that affects each other, even though we can find stronger ties between single "perspectives" and single "network layers," for instance, the Transaction Cost Theory and the genesis of "production networks."

Distinguishing the three different networks, I follow Johannisson (1987b). He considers networks a universal organizing vehicle. It is important for him to also include moral and affective aspects in social analysis. "A conceptional scheme concerning social-exchange networks must include explicit concern for the affective dimension" (Johannisson, 1987b, p. 9). The network approach certainly does have the potential for conceptualizing even these phenomena. He follows a study of Kanter on the rise and decline of utopian communities, suggesting three potential commitment-building elements in collective effort: instrumentality, affection, and shared values. They represent the basis of three kinds of networks: the production network, the personal network, and the symbolic network (Gustaffson & Johannisson, 1984, p. 11).

In "arenas" these networks become established. The production network is typically built in the marketplace, for example, at business meetings and fairs, or through trade associations. Mostly considered as a model of formal organization, bounded rationality as instrumental commitment is expected to guide coupling and decoupling.

The cultural network is built through the community. It is based on norms and values that encourage common or discourage unorthodox choices of network linkages. It manifests the beliefs and attitudes that become the "software" of individual behavior. It has to be reflected as a context when individual and social changes have to be initiated.

The personal network follows no rule as it emerges tie by tie. Affection leads to casual choices of both arenas and realized network ties. Among the three networks proposed here, the personal network is the only one that is truly personal in the sense that the nodes, the individuals, are irreplaceable (Johannisson, 1987b). The network-building process, therefore, because of its emotional content, is uncontrollable and irrational. This indicates that the personal network has the greatest potential for both innovative and destructive processes within social structures.

FIGURE 7.2.   MULTIPLE NETWORKS AND ARENAS CONNECTING THE VALUE
AND INSTRUMENTAL STRUCTURE

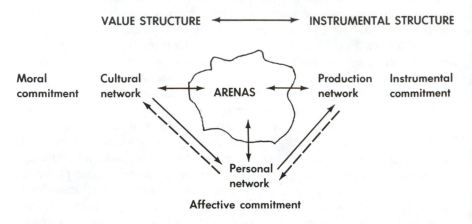

Network Layers

Figure 7.2 corresponds to Weick's image of how organized activity emerges from the cultural network framing the personal network which in turn conditions what kind of production networks will emerge. This chain is reciprocal and reflects a circle of development characterized by a spiral. The network concept allows us to achieve deeper insight into these terms. The acceptance of "network thinking" can affect physical and psychological "network design" and vice versa. Using network as a concept for analyzing and understanding organizational interdependencies, it is able to change the "mental map" as a prerequisite of change. The following section discusses aspects of different networks.

Production networks. Miles, for example, introduces a "mental picture," to give a glimpse of certain organizational and productive networks: "A piece of ice hockey equipment, designed in Scandinavia, engineered in the U.S. to meet the requirements of the large U.S. and Canadian market, manufactured in Korea and distributed through a multinational market network with initial distribution from Japan" (Miles, 1989, p. 17). The classical hierarchy is dismissed. Development, production, and distribution become an "event," in which different units in different countries are cooperating. Miles and Snow (1986) introduce the diagram shown as Figure 7.3.

The broker's task is to establish the proper network, which depends on the organizational task. For Miles, networking means the fast coordination and accumulation of persons, goods, and informa-

FIGURE 7.3.   DYNAMIC NETWORK ORGANIZATION

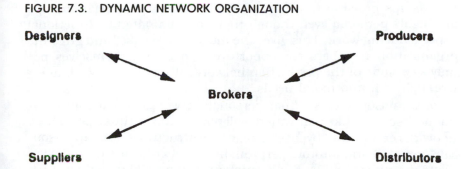

tion as the key determinants of organizational flexibility. The broker role is not necessarily independent and fixed. The broker position can be fulfilled by a single networking party, but not necessarily. Katz (1980) points out that it could be a team, that the central role in a network can shift.

These organizational networks mostly address interorganizational exchange. The point of interest is the coordinated cooperation between different units that constitute the network. Spot transactions are the exception; exchange relations with a lasting perspective are intended. "For us, industrial markets are characterized by lasting relationships among firms because such relationships can reduce costs of exchange and production and can promote knowledge development and change" (Johanson & Mattson, 1987, p. 46).

Thus, networks as organizations derive their advantage through more open and flexible settings than hierarchies. Because networks are based on mutual exchanges in the past, time, and even money, intensive investments can take place. A common perspective of time and modes and exchange is needed to support the trust-building process. Trust and low costs of control become the strategic advantage for the partners.

Personal networks. So far the discussion of organization has been oriented toward the production network. Nevertheless, the affective commitment for personal network creation is often important to support the production network. It is to be noted that orientation among and in firms is based on orientation among individuals. "Power, perceived expertise, perceived trustworthiness and social bonds are often person-specific rather than firm-specific" (Thorelli, 1986, p. 47). In other words, personal networks often carry the production network.[7] Examples of this phenomenon are

---

[7] This process, however, represents the hen and the egg problem as it is intertwined.

friendships growing in a productive network. These relationships are highly personal even though they are dominated by functional aspects during work. This gives the individual "sense" and gives the organization members the opportunity to realize themselves not only as a node of the production network. It relates to social, affective, cultural, and moral needs.[8]

Johannisson stresses that personal networks can mobilize dynamic resources like motivation, will power, and enthusiasm. These networks enable the "bypassing of formal structures" (Johannisson, 1987a, p. 60) and improve performance. "Networks are quite invisible to the eye and difficult to document. But we all know that much of the work to any system is done through informal and invisible networks, rather than through formal visible authority structures" (Fombrun, 1982, p. 280). The concept of networks can reflect on this organizational reality. Traditionally, informal structures in organizations were viewed as inconsistent with task accomplishment and the organization goal. The functional pattern of informal structures is often overlooked. Tichy argues that informal and formal structures "should be treated together, as each emerging structure (and prescribed structure) has its own functional logic" (Tichy & Fombrun, 1979, p. 926), and he recommends that "people must be allowed to improvise and rely on personal networks to coordinate and carry out their work" (p. 931).

Cultural networks. Cultural aspects are always involved in social exchange. Thus, it is important to perceive theses aspects as potentially helpful and not as antagonistic. This is not easy because the cultural network stays mostly latent.

The interest in focusing culture in corporations as an important element for social development arises with the increasing turbulence of the environment. As structural settings failed, nonstructural elements were identified as important in shaping social order. Culture is an intrinsic prerequisite for organizations. Johannisson argues that culture combines stability with a tremendous potential for change (Johannisson, 1987). If organization members share the values of a certain culture, the energy needed for "convincing" them is obsolete. The central processes take place intentionally or unconsciously; however, it has to be assumed that only little influence can be exerted on the emerging culture (Schein, personal communication, February 1984). Ouchi (1980) is more optimistic establishing

---

[8] "Sociologists, in particular point out that economic relationships also contain elements of mutual trust and exchange of social and cultural kind" (Johannisson, 1987, p. 43).

and internally marketing a set of values and attitudes concerning the task of the organization.

Corporate culture has to be functional. The "clan" as a governance structure is ideal when goal incongruence is low and performance ambiguity is high. "National cultural characteristics dominate corporate cultural properties" (Johannisson, 1987b, p. 7). We can find some validity for that statement when comparing organization life in different countries. In Italy, for instance, organization culture looks different than Britain's or Japan's. Corporations reflect certain values, norms, and moral standards emergent in society. Thus, the different social levels are contingent with respect to each other.

Objectives

It is important to observe that the objectives introduced in Table 7.2 do not correlate identically to the related perspectives and networks on the corresponding line. However, they display stronger corresponding ties in horizontal rubrics than objectives, perspectives, and networks appearing on different lines.

Performance. In general, networks increase the potential of perception and are able to generate information. Weick points out "that loosely coupled systems preserve many independent sensing elements and therefore know their environment better than is true for more tightly coupled systems which have fewer externally constrained, independent elements" (Weick, 1976, p. 6). The use of networks, either productive or personal, supplies direct information. If particular information is not directly available, it is often possible to acquire it indirectly through second-order zones. Networks supply a capacity to cope with uncertainty and complexity. This strongly relates to the capacity of networks to generate information.[9]

Further, the use of networks serves as a control mechanism itself. As networks offer a variety of information, this multisided view prevents the observer from unreflected use of one information source only. The use of networks supports the "washing out" of old rigid settings in organizations. Through interconnections, multiple

---

[9] Much concern is made on the ability of organizations to cope with complexity. Willke (1989) states that social development is strongly connected with increasing complexity. There is a need to establish contingent organizations that are able to exist in complex environments. In order to generate the necessary variety and responsiveness in organizations Ochsenbauer (1988) recommends networks.

perspectives can replace preexisting constricted patterns. Empirical research has been performed on diffusion of new technology in companies. It was found that "social networking is an aid in adapting from one technology to another and that the organization which can adopt more quickly and more effectively has a strategic advantage" (Kochen, 1988, p. 19).

Additionally, we note that informal subsystems are better suited to cope with crises than formal systems.[10] Crises often demand a quick generation of new actions that do not exist in the normal repertoire of actions. Justification of action, which often is an element of formal organization, is too costly during crises.

Individual growth. Individual growth reflects on the goals and objectives of people (Friedlander, 1974). The network concept entails aspects that seem to support the need for self-actualization. It consists of the following elements:

1. Authority is decentralized; competence and the level of information are the dominant criteria of task distribution. Positions on any "blue print" often ignore this demand.
2. Corporate policy and corporate limits no longer carry exclusive meaning. Exchange relations become more responsive and normal at all levels of the organization. The former centralizing forces do not have the intention to close the organization.
3. Persons tend to interact as equals, more so than as subordinates and superiors.
4. Structures in networks are more polycentric than monocentric.

For Hine (1970), networks offer precisely the structure which seems to her consistent with the vision of the "Global Village," "debureaucratization," and "rehumanization."

Social development. The classical goals of organization development—"Performance" and "Individual Growth"—are, of course, mostly achieved at the organizational and individual levels. However, these levels are embedded in a social interconnectedness which can be described as society. Thus, the achievements of the goals of OD are related to the encompassing collective conditions.

---

[10] "Informal systems of coordination have many virtues. They tend to be flexible and adaptive. The disruptive effects of innovation in a formal hierarchy, because of its tightly coupled interdependencies, are avoided in the more loosely coupled, flat, informal system of coordination. Such informal systems are problem oriented and pragmatic. They are self organizing in the sense that they respond to the effects of experience rather that to the 'a priori' demands of organizational designers" (Chisholm, 1989, p. 12).

There is a need for compatability between different system levels.[11] However, individuals and organizations cannot ignore the values of the general environment. They affect them and can improve them through their example.[12]

This example shows that organizations have an interest in the conditions of their outer environment. Presently, this interest seems to increase.

Governmental policies which used to be considered as responsible for the design of political, social, and cultural settings are no longer satisfying. There are two possible solutions in regard to this power vacuum. It can either be left as such or it can be filled by interest groups or other discernible systems. Still, many corporations and organizations object to this idea when they are confronted with this new situation in society. However, other organizations reproach the government that its measures are not extensive enough to cope with present problems. Particularly, the big corporations are motivated to codetermine the general framework. In some cultures this even goes so far that they proclaim the business community as the authority to carry a new "Ordnungspolitik," because the government has failed to face the problems.[13] As relatively big units in society, they have higher motivation to engage on a societal level than smaller units (Olson, 1965).

Even though organizations are more and more inclined to occupy the role of the "social or holistic entrepreneur," they also often fail. In many cases they even misuse their influence. Thus, it is necessary that Western pluralistic societies generate new ideas, attitudes, and values. Individuals and institutions contribute to the genesis of

---

[11] We often can observe incompatibility when people and organizations from Western countries have to cope with an environment and attitudes in different cultures and societies. For instance, it is difficult for a Western company to send a female project engineer to the Arabic countries, because it is considered that women are not obliged to do business. Another example is a Western electronic plant in South Africa where apartheid also effects organizational settings. It is difficult to distribute positions in the plant in regard to performing in abilities and performance. Giving colored people leading positions, even though they are qualified for doing this particular job, can lead to opposition from white people on the production level.

[12] We can observe that the company mentioned above established a corporate culture in the South African plant, which abolished apartheid in the organization. A culture of cooperation and appreciation between colored and white people emerged. It improved the performance as well as individual well-being. This culture also radiated to the outer environment and enhanced the diffusion of understanding between conflicting groups.

[13] Alfred Herrhausen, former CEO of Deutsche Bank AG, has been a representative of this position.

multiple aspects of life. These aspects are developed in cultural, personal, and productive networks. With that in mind we can view the cultural network as a strong influence having changed the attitude towards ecology in Germany and elsewhere in Europe. Even though the individual actions concerning ecological consciousness are still very incomplete, this concern has become a cultural feature acting at the individual level, for example, not to throw away glass and paper, using water and energy more consciously, and so forth.

This section stressed that the dimension of collective improvement is not only a value itself, but is also a prerequisite for performance and individual growth. Furthermore, distinguishing different networks can improve the insights and handling of reality. In the following section I try to illuminate the concept of networks as a means of improvement. The cognitive and instrumental dimensions are discussed, pragmatic, practical concepts are introduced, to make networking real.

NETWORK MANAGEMENT

We saw that networks and networking became an approach to cope with higher complexity and turbulent environments. Nevertheless, it is unclear how networks can be established or how networking among individuals can be fostered. There are many reasons for this:

1. Thinking in networks is mostly unfamiliar as it transcends present cognitive limits that have been established in a long-lasting process of socialization. Tearing down these limits confronts people with openness and insecurity which they often do not like.
2. Network building as an emergent process is often suppressed or at least kept within limits. People in organizations are anxious because of the open and apparently uncontrollable metamorphosis, that is, the development of new structures/networks. People are afraid to lose their power bases.
3. The emerging of networks is often unplanned and spontaneous. This prevents use of conventional frameworks. Without this knowledge it is difficult to define settings conventionally and to effectively make use of the new structures in turbulent social environments.

Network understanding and network abilities are often expected from individuals, even though these expectations are not explicitly communicated. When vacant positions in organizations have to be filled, the capacity to think in interdependencies is often viewed as an individual ability which cannot be influenced, developed, and improved. This attitude also holds when various categories of leadership are discussed. It is common to believe that leadership abilities are exclusively personal intrinsic features that cannot be changed. However, this seems to ignore the relevant potential of networks in this context.

In considering organizational aspects that can support networking, we note that two interlocked levels need to be examined. First, the "mental map" often tends to oppose networks, being rooted in past "standard" constructions. Second, the "institutional settings" themselves are often rigid and counterproductive to networking processes. However, these levels are interdependent so that we can assume that the change in institutional setting will affect the mental map of the organization member, and vice versa.

Mental Map

Emphasis is placed on those aspects that are personal, even though these are often determined or affected by environmental forces. For the person, network relations are often unconscious and incidental. Reflection on one's own "network setting" is often lacking. Even though these "network settings" may be unconscious, they have their own rationality which is often reflected in personal history and socialization. The capability to create networks and to be involved in networks may initially differ among individuals.[14] The impact of local and temporal restrictions on the genesis of the individual network setting is to be kept in mind. However, mostly the size of the personal networks and their active potentials are underestimated.

The concept of networks transforms the classical understanding of hierarchy. The need to establish contingent structures with reference to the environment also includes coping with individual settings of persons who feel offended by more open and flexible structures. Probably, it takes time until people feel comfortable to think

---

[14] One very interesting experience is the different culture and understanding of former West and East German persons. Even though they speak the same language, communication between them often has been clouded by various interpretations. This is due to their history. Different systems with different scopes for the individual lead to different perceptions. It is interesting to recognize that psychologists in former East Germany perceive grades of "personal deformation" among the population, which they attribute to the former repressive regime. This is not the place to compare and evaluate forms of deformation in these two systems. However, focus is on the bases which allow various scopes for development in various settings.

in terms of network interdependencies. Therefore, it is helpful to guide development toward networks by measures which "take people up where they are." That means that the establishing of networks is a process that involves opening up the "cognitive map" first, that employees can appreciate the potentials of networks for their own and the organization development. On the other hand, it is also necessary to communicate a need to reform present mechanistic organizations.

This process will require intense communication. Communication is not only essential for the process itself, it is also most important for the concept of networks. This includes all measures of communication, whether oral or written, direct or mediated.[15]

Institutional Setting

The extension of communication technology that we can presently observe in industrialized countries seems to constitute a fundamental force in supplying a supportive environment for networks. Counterproductive to the existence of this technology, the access for using it is often restricted. The ability to continue organization development and to cope with turbulent environments depends on information access, which is not preselected by hierarchical order, that is, order which has been introduced to rationalize information processing while often being overtaken and made obsolete by the development of the actual situation.

The abandonment of former structures of information selection can affect performance in the short run. But it seems to me important to foster an information-processing climate that leaves the selection decision where the "action is."[16]

To continue, I would like to distinguish two levels for further discussions; the intraorganizational and interorganizational levels.

---

[15] Weisbord focused on an interesting aspect. He suggests, that leaders have certain qualities. These qualities seem to me also valid for "networkers": "They focus attention on worthy aspirations; they mobilize energy by involving others; they seem willing to face the unknown without answers" (Weisbord, 1987, p. 16).

[16] A very interesting example was mentioned by Sievers. He distinguishes four levels of management. He starts with Management I: Self-management; Management II: The management in a group; Management III: The management between groups; Management IV: The management of the organization in its environment. Principally, however, every person is able to manage. This concept brought up that the worker on the production level is the expert in processing certain material, because that is his daily job. Thus, he is the appropriate specialist to purchase the material for the company. This experiment was a great success.

On both levels networking takes place. Networks at these different levels are interconnected. In this context, I will discuss some practical aspects that seem to be supportive of the diffusion of the network concept.

Intraorganizational. Processes that distribute work projects to the most competent team or member in the organization can induce better results. This improvement can be achieved in work quality, productivity, and efficiency, and in the motivation of the organization members. This could be organized through "organizational bidding processes." Similar to "public tendering," an organizational authority (this authority can be established in various ways; its design can range from a position for a single person to a general meeting) receives proposals from different work teams. These proposals may offer a suggested approach or solution for a particular work project. Additionally, each group introduces arguments of why they consider themselves to be the group which "fits" best with the task (Tichy, 1981).

This is one procedure that can enhance entrepreneurial consciousness in organizations. The tendency to establish "profit centers"[17] is also a means to foster responsibility and engagement by organization members. Beyond "Leverage Buy Outs" and "Spin Offs" externalizing entrepreneurial activity, an alternative could be the establishment of "entrepreneurial islands," units that become established under the "roof" of a corporation with internal start-up support.[18] These units are loosely coupled in the corporation and can unfold more easily when combining self-reliance with the access to staff and organizational slack of the "roof," in context of specified resources.

There is consensus that organization design should encourage open coalition formation, overt bargaining, and fair conflict.[19] Open conflict and dissent is a minimal condition for development, even

---

[17] Freimuth, however, criticizes that systems of cost control are often counterproductive to the whole performance of organization. These concepts may lead to single optimizing of "cost islands" without any consciousness for the interdependent effects and costs. It is very difficult to establish cost systems that are able to reflect on the multiple interdependencies. Thus, there is evidence that nonstructural concepts as corporate culture are supportive elements.

[18] Very interesting models have been realized in Sweden. See Johannisson (1987b), Johanson and Mattson (1987).

[19] Further discussion exists on the realization of democratic values in organizations and corporations. Particularly, social scientists argue that there is no irreproachable explanation for why organizations should not also carry democratic systems. Later in this chapter I will also take position on the cost argument.

though consensus is necessary to maintain the ability to act. Even in present mechanistic organizations it makes sense to incorporate opposing elements, furthering innovative processes (Olson, 1965). Some organizations may even elect their supervisors,[20] frequently changing "power center" by elections. Another supportive element for network building is the transfer of people. Often trainee programs involve this element. Tichy (1981, p. 242) urges that "an organization should plan transfers strategically and attend to linking the transferees into relevant networks" (Tichy, 1981, p. 242).

Modern organizations have the capacity to function as "sense-seeking systems," some companies are following this track, for example, Volkswagen AG.[21] They function in part as not only "think tanks" in new technology and product development, but they also strive for societal and value change as well.

Networks are based on a long-run perspective. People prefer to use the "voice mode." The "exit mode" becomes less attractive. Therefore, trust emerges as an essential ingredient of networks to keep them going and to facilitate attainment of personal and task goals. Lack of trust limits the potential of networks to unfold their multiple exchanges of information, goods, and affects, and increases transaction costs. "Being able to generate trust, therefore, is the fundamental entrepreneurial skill to lower those costs and make the existence of the network economically feasible" (Jarillo, 1988, p. 36).

Jarillo also suggests two aspects that can support trust building. It is important to carefully choose the networking partner. The emergence of trust is more likely if people have similar values and motivations and if people can "relate" to each other (Jarillo, 1988). Focus on partner history and reputation is worthwhile.

Clearly the development of networks requires time. "Social exchange relations evolve in a slow process, starting with minor transactions in which little trust is required because little risk is involved and in which both partners can prove their trustworthiness, enabling them to expand their relation and to engage in major transaction" (Johannisson, 1987, p. 37).

Thorelli (1986) asserts that trust is a very important ingredient in network building. In line with Kants "categoric imperative," Thorelli defines trust:

An assumption or reliance on the part of A that if either A or B encounters a problem in the fulfillment of his implicit or explicit

---

[20] See the software company PSI in Berlin.
[21] See research of Volkswagen on transportation and other societal issues carried by either the Volkswagen AG or the Volkswagen Stiftung.

transactional obligations, B may be counted on to do what A would do if B's resources were at A's disposal. Observe that trust dissolves the need to specify unforeseeable consequences, for it is assumed that the decision rule to be followed will be identical to my own decision rule. (Thorelli, 1986, p. 36)

Most simply, networks describe exchanges. Therefore, local and temporal opportunities have to be established. As Johannisson and others (Kirsch, 1988) suggest, "arenas" are essential for networking. They constitute a basis for exchange. On the cultural or community level, settings from the marketplace to congregations can be regarded as arenas.

Networking can also be supported by offering opportunities for interaction. The concept of canteens, cafeterias, and shared meals in diverse groups is not to be underestimated as means for the distribution of information. Some companies provide a "forum" that can be used by employees to discuss professional or personal problems. The informal aspect of club activities, whether sports- or culture-oriented, is also to be considered. "People who should communicate with each other should be located near each other, physical layouts can bring interdependent people together, regulate traffic flow, and foster affective relationships which match task relationship" (Tichy, 1981, p. 241).

More and more interest has been shown with regard to architectural solutions that might enhance networking. The main effort then is on the structural support to meet each other, when moving among offices during a work day. A style often chosen for university campuses seems presently to be very fashionable and functional in a perspective of information diffusion and network enhancement in a variety of organizations. Generally, "for organizational change it is very important not only to change the superstructure of organizations often represented by the blueprint. Without attending to underlying political-economic conditions can be successful only within a restricted range" (Benson, 1975, p. 248).

Interorganizational. Principally, all measures for intraorganizational network building are valid for interorganizational settings as well. When remembering Figure 6.3, we become aware of the relations of interorganizational networks. Their establishment often depends strongly on the background of certain organizational units and its members. For instance, departments have set up many contacts within the environment of the organization. Usually, purchasing and sales departments have particular knowledge of the branch, the spectrum of suppliers, competitors, and related branches and enterprises. Associations play a significant role in the maintenance of these contacts and the distribution of information. These associations may be very firm-specific. Also, regional clustering can determine their formation. Conventions, exhibitions, and fairs may offer the context to maintain and to expand interorganizational networks.

Furthermore, interorganizational networks may be based on former experiences and involvements of individuals. Organizational members have their contacts to former peers. Being sent abroad may also be an opportunity and challenge to build up new contacts and to gain new perspectives on the former network setting.

Interorganizational network building may depend strongly on the involvement of different persons from inside and outside the organization projects. A certain degree of mobility and information exchange among these people may be fundamental. Consequently, organizations need to give time, scope, and resources to people.

OUTLOOK

So far we have examined the concept of networks. After defining an understanding of networks, we focused on its contribution to organization development. Therefore, we distinguished several network layers (production, personal, and cultural). Besides the classical objectives—"performance" and "individual growth"—we also assumed "social development" as important. Cultural networks are considered as supportive of social development. The section on network management tries to illuminate several ways to make networks feasible for the individual, organizational, and societal level. Particularly, cognitive aspects and institutional settings were viewed as critical for network development.

The network concept is based on interaction and exchange. It enlarges the understanding of the flow of goods, values, and affection within the organization as well as outside the organization. The environment of enterprises consists not only of suppliers and customers, it is also influenced by many other interdependencies on the individual, organizational, and societal level. The network concept may reflect these interdependencies more contingently. As it enlarges the perspective of organization reality, it generates complexity that is preliminary to analyze and design organizational action in an increasingly complex world.

The openness and the perspective potential of the concept emphasizes process and structural diversity, fostering communication in organization. Thus, the danger of the "black holes" in perception is reduced, allowing to break up perceptual filters and to redefine situations (Kirsch, 1988). In the understanding of Hedberg, networking allows learning. "Learning in this sense is discovery. Learners discover themselves and their environment; these discoverings lead to comprehension of reasons beyond events, and ultimately to mental maps of relevant aspects of the environment" (Hedberg, 1981, p. 4). Thus, the network concept stands for the improvement of carrying potentials for perception and design of internal and external relations between the organization and its environment and its contribution to long-range processes of consciousness building, learning, and development.

However, further research on networks is affected by the confusing use of the network metaphor. Still, the term "network" is used in different and even contradictory ways. Describing it with the network metaphor itself, the links between the different positions are lacking. Additionally, the concept of networks is very abstract. Transparency into networks is often hard to gain, which makes it difficult to distinguish networks in reality. A main point of critique is that the network concept does not answer who is carrying network transformation. Therefore, the explanation of impulses in networks is a question to be addressed in the future. The network concept seems to be promising for more intensive research. Particularly fruitful may be the reflection on practical experiences.

REFERENCES

Benson, J. K. (1975). The interoganizations network as a political economy. *Administrative Science Quarterly, 20,* 229–249.

Boissevain, J. (1974). *Friends of friends: Networks, manipulators and coaltions.* New York: St. Martin's Press

Borys, B., & Jemison, D. B. (1987). *Hybrid organizations as strategic alliances. Theoretical and practical issues in organizational combinations* (No. 951). Unpublished paper, Graduate School of Business, Stanford University.

Chisholm, D. W. (1989). *Coordination without hierarchy. Informal structures in multiorganizational systems.* Berkeley: University of California Press.

Emery, F. (1982). New perspectives on the world of work. Sociotechnical foundations for a new social order? *Human Relation, 35,* 1095–1122.

Fombrun, C. (1982). Strategies for network research in organizations. *Academy of management review, 7,* 280–291.

Friedlander, F., & Brown, D. (1974). Organization development. *Annual Review of Psychology, 25,* 313–341.

Gustaffson, B. A., & Johannisson, B. (1984, June 26–30). *Local business cultures—A network perspective.* Paper presented at the First International Conference on Organizational Symbolism and Corporate Culture, University of Lund, Sweden.

Harris, P. R. (1985). *Management in transition: Transforming managerial practices and organizational strategies for new work culture.* San Francisco: Jossey-Bass.

Hedberg, B. (1981). How organizations learn and unlearn. In P. C. Nystroem & W. H. Starbuck (Eds.), *Handbook of organizational design.* London: Oxford University Press.

Hine, V., & Gerlach, L. (1970). *People, power, change.* Bloomington, IN: University of Indiana Press.

Jarillo, J. C. (1988). On strategic networks. *Strategic Management Journal, 9,* 31–41.

Johannisson, B. (1987a). Anarchists and organizers: Entrepreneurs in a network perspective. *International Studies of Management & Organization, 17*(1), 49–63,

Johannisson, B. (1987b). Beyond processes and structure: Social exchange networks. *International Studies of Management & Organization, 17,* 3–23.

Johanson, J., & Mattson, L. G. (1987). Interorganizational relations in industrial systems: A network approach compared with the transaction-cost-approach. *International Studies of Management & Organization, 17,* 34–48.

Katz, D. (1980, Fall). The network-overlay: Helping large bureaucracies do things better. *Bureaucrat,* pp. 24–29.

Kirsch, W. (1988). *Die fortschrittsfaehige organisation.* Unveroeffentlichtes Manuskript. Muenchen: Kirsch.

Kochen, M. (1988). *Social network for successful adoption of technology.* Ann Arbor, MI: University Michigan, Graduate School of Business Administration, Working Papers Pamphlet Collection.

Leveson, I. (1986). The phenomenon of strategic collaboration. *Directors and Board, 10,* 18–25.

Luhmann, N. (1984). *Soziale systeme, grundriss einer allgemeinen theorie.* Frankfurt: Suhrkamp.

Maturana, H. R., & Varela, F. J. (1980). Autopoiesis and cognition. The realization of the living. Boston: Cambridge University Press.

McInnis, N. (1984). The tao of networking. *The Futurist, 18,* 18–19.

Miles, R. E., & Snow, C. C. (1986). Organizations: New concepts for new forms. *California Management Review, 27*(3), 62–73.

Ochsenbauer, C. (1988). *Organisatorische alternativen zur hierarchie.* Muenchen: Kirsch.

Olson, M. (1965). *The logic of collective action.* New Haven, CT: Yale University Press.

Ouchi, W. (1980). Markets, bureaucracies, and clans. *Administrative Science Quarterly, 25,* 129–141.

Schein, E. (1984, February). Soll und kann man eine Organisations-Kultur veraendern? *Gdi impuls,* pp. 31–43.

Schenk, M. (1984). *Soziale netzwerke und kommunikation*. Tuebingen: Mohr.

Thorelli, H. B. (1986). Networks: Between markets and hierarchies. *Strategic Management Journal, 7,* 37–51.

Tichy, N. M., & Frombrun, C. (1979). Network analysis in organizational settings. *Human Relations, 32,* 923–965.

Tichy, N. M. (1981). Networks in organizations. In P. Nystroem & W. Starbuck (Eds.), *Handbook of organizational Design* (Vol. 1, pp. 225–249). Oxford: Oxford University Press.

Ulrich, H., & Probst, G. (Eds.). (1984). *Self-organizations and management of social systems, insights, promises, doubts and questions.* Berlin: Springer.

Weick, K. E. (1976). Educational organizations as loosely coupled systems. *Administrative Science Quarterly, 21,* 1–19.

Weisbord, M. (1978). *Organizational diagnosis, A workbook of theory and practice.*

Weisbord, M. (1987). Towards third-wave managing and consulting. *Organizational Dynamics, 15*(3), 5–24.

Willke, II. (1989). *Systemtheorie entwickelter gesellschaften.* Weinheim, Germany: Juventa.

Wimmer, R. (1989). Die steuerung komplexer organisationen. Ein reformulierungsveruch der fuehrungsproblematik aus systemischer sicht. In K. Sander (Ed.), *Politische prozesse in organisationen.* Berlin: Springer.

8

Trusting Relationships, Empowerment, and the Conditions That Produce Truth Telling

Samuel A. Culbert and John J. McDonough
University of California, Los Angeles

As much as it embodies any single emphasis, Organization Development is the applied science of helping people to truthfully and openly communicate and to exchange on a timely basis. Almost always management's call for OD results when confronting critical problems that cannot be solved due to a lack of candor. Management might be concerned that work associates lack the give-and-take communications required for developing a realistic view of markets, product, personnel, and/or organizational capabilities. It might be concerned that work associates are excessively political and deliberately do not exchange information that could help another department to function more effectively. Or it might be concerned that work associates are intentionally clandestine and misleading in characterizing the personal interests and stakes of those who are party to a disagreement, their own interests and stakes as well as those of others. In today's managerial world, conventional wisdom prescribes the timely telling of the truth as crucial to teamwork and organizational effectiveness and holds that no management can be effective for long while something less than the truth is being told.

But what does truth telling actually entail? How does one gauge the crossover points where interpreting the facts, or not revealing some of the facts, becomes materially less than telling the truth? What is an acceptable deviation from the truth when one feels his or her first obligation is to work toward, or to preserve, some higher-order end? Goffman (1961) has shown us that truth telling proceeds differently behind the scenes than in front of them, and Bok (1978, 1982) has emphasized the difference between telling the truth and withholding it. But neither has provided a framework for extracting the truth when one most needs to hear it told.

In the public realm, controversial examples of subordinating scrupulous truth telling to "higher order" ends are widespread and popularized. White House press secretary Larry Speakes (1988) admitted that he "manufactured" statements he thought President Reagan should have made and intentionally represented them to the press as the truth. Secretary of State George Schultz (1987) asked the American people to look leniently on the mistruths and misleading statements Assistant Secretary of State Elliot Abrams made in a closed meeting of the Senate Foreign Relations Committee in response to questions about the United States' involvement in Nicaragua. Bill McGowan, Chairman and CEO of MCI Communications Corporation, approved his deputies issuing innocuous and obscuring statements about his health when he took medical leave to undergo heart transplant surgery out of his higher-order concern that speculators might overreact and drive down the price of the MCI stock (Bennett, 1988). In everyday spheres, the use of "higher-order" objectives to justify not telling the truth are even more flagrantly evoked.

In theory truth telling at work seems like a very straightforward issue: Either someone tells the truth or he or she does not. In practice, however, truth telling is seldom simple. It is complex and it quickly takes on many dimensions and nuances. Everyone knows that people provide one another *versions* of the truth. Everyone knows that most *straightforward statements of the truth* are usually biased and self-serving. Everyone knows that there are *degrees of truth* and there are *incomplete truths*.

But even though everyone knows and understands all of this, we find that people who are denied the truth react quite emotionally. They become indignant, moralistic, rageful, and even punitive and revengeful once they discern that the truth has been withheld or that some other rendition was intentionally provided. This is in spite of the fact that everyone also knows that all so-called *truthful statements* must be scrutinized and interpreted for underlying meaning and motivation.

This chapter examines some key issues that complicate truth telling at work. It develops a model that can be used (a) to promote truth telling, (b) to comprehend the type of truth telling that is actually being carried out, and (c) to discern the conditions that are required for a valid discussion and exchange of "truths" from the conditions that lead directly to withholding, misrepresentation, and deceit. Ultimately, the quality of truth telling that is being exchanged relates to the level of trust that exists between the people who are transacting it. And ultimately, both the inclination to seek the truth and the willingness to tell the truth are related to the empowerment needs of the people who are interacting. Accordingly, we begin the explication of our truth-telling model by examining issues bearing on the basis of trusting relationships and on the empowerment needs that motivate people both to seek the truth and to selectively represent it.

TRUST

In organizations there is a fundamental premise that relates trusting relationships to the effectiveness of people, to the effectiveness of work units, and to the effectiveness of entire systems (Gibb, 1978). It's a premise in which we have always believed and, with more grey hair and experience, we maintain in our consciousness with increasing strength and conviction. In fact, we have gotten to the point where we now consider trusting relationships to be the most efficient tool known to modern management. We have seen countless instances where the presence of trusting relationships allowed flawed plans and imperfect systems to work out fine. We have also seen countless instances where the lack of trusting relationships caused the best formulated plans to go awry, and the best conceived systems to turn sour.

This is all quite straightforward. Get people to trust you, be worthy of their confidence, and they will believe in your guidance, they will give you the benefit of the doubt, they will cooperate with you, they will follow your lead, and they will stand behind you when your critics are on the verge of swamping your best efforts with their negative judgments.

But how often does one find trusting relationships within organizations these days? In our experience the answer is "Not often enough." Instead of finding people involved in real trusting relationships, too often we find people involved in merely the affectations of one. Some of these people are on the receiving end, apparently possessing such a strong desire to trust that they can be easily deceived into thinking that others are trustworthy when these others are not. Other people are on the sending end, possessing such a strong desire to be trusted that they can look sincere and portray themselves as trustworthy while energetically pursuing their own interests at another person's expense. People apparently have such a strong desire to form trusting relationships that they readily accept the *cosmetics* of trust in place of the real thing.

We have spent substantial time thinking about what makes people trustworthy. And we mean deservedly trustworthy, in contrast to the cosmetics of trust that are so prevalent in management circles these days. In fact, whenever we get a chance, we ask managers "Whom do you trust?" and then inquire into the character and basis of that trust by asking them "Why?"

In response to our questions, three trust topics repeatedly come into focus. First, people talk about trusting someone to do a job competently—which ultimately translates into "I believe this other person will perform his or her job as I expect it to be performed, in a way that is good for me, without my having to constantly check up on him or her." Many people qualify their response by adding, "Of course, if I later find out that the job was not performed as I had reason to expect or in a way that was not good for me—what was done either blocks me from being effective or appearing that way to others—than I am going to have problems trusting that person any longer."

Second, people talk about trusting someone to look out for their interests—which ultimately implies that a second individual understands enough about the conditions they need established in order to perform competently and to be professionally successfully, organizationally secure, financially whole, and emotionally fulfilled and that this second individual is sufficiently committed to making sure that the needs and interests of the first person are given fair consideration. Of course, unless the first individual feels that a second individual understands his or her goals, resources, sensitivities, and interests well enough, then the first person is not going to trust that other person.

Third, people talk about trusting another person to tell them the truth—which ultimately translates to "I trust you to truthfully answer the questions I ask *and* to tell me what I need to know, whether or not I think to ask the right question." Of course, if a second individual doesn't comprehend enough about what a first individual needs to know and why he or she needs to hear it straight, then that second individual is going to have major difficulties providing the information that the first person is actually seeking.

Each of these responses has a common core. People want to be seen realistically as they actually are, not as someone else wants them to be, *and* they want others to respect their needs and interests, and to look out for those interests even while these others are looking out for their own. Thus, we find that people trust those individuals who make it possible for them to succeed, not just in ways that fit with those other individuals' special interests, but in ways that fit with what they see as their personal inclinations and special talents and capacities.

EMPOWERMENT

Unlike the niche-seekers of the past, we find that in today's organizations almost everyone seeks a position of personal and organizational *empowerment*. By empowerment we mean that people seek a unique work orientation that (a) utilizes what they see as their strengths and best abilities, (b) is based on a definition of the job that they see as both personally meaningful and organizationally relevant, and (c) is accurately perceived, respected, and valued by others in their organization. People who feel empowered function with feelings of high energy and spirited commitment because in their minds they are working in personally meaningful ways producing product that is important to the organization. What's more, they believe others are going to comprehend what they are accomplishing and appreciate them for doing so.

In organizations, people trust those whose orientations and modes of interacting leave them feeling empowered. Conversely, people distrust and resent those others whose own ways of seeing things and being effective clash with their ways of performing well and feeling competent. That is, people distrust those whose ways of being empowered appear competitive with their own. For instance, managers who feel secure with tight controls often distrust peers and subordinates whose natural ways of operating produce loose structures and flexible operating plans. Likewise, people who are uncomfortable with conflict often distrust those whose ways of operating and achieving conceptual clarity entail taking adversarial stands.

Once we assume that people want to function with feelings of empowerment, it becomes easy to identify the specific types of behavior that produce trust. People trust those who inquire into who they are individually, understand what they want to accomplish, comprehend the distinctive resources they possess and how they plan to use those resources in getting from where they are today to where they want to be tomorrow, and who demonstrate respect for them and their right to seek what they are trying to achieve by telling them the *truth*. In this context, telling the "truth" involves substantially more than merely providing an honest response to the questions asked. It entails making a response that reflects insight into who the other person is and what that person him- or herself wants to know, and it demonstrates respect for that individual's right to have the information he or she is seeking.

TRUTH TELLING

We find that people take tremendous "liberties" and grant themselves wide latitudes in truth telling when they don't respect a truth seeker, when they don't know much about that individual and the needs that underlie the specific questions he or she is asking, or when they fear that telling the truth will place themselves or their projects at risk. This is the case even for people who pride themselves on having the highest integrity.

In considering what one has the right to expect from prospective truth tellers, the issues of trust and empowerment stand out. When a trusting relationship is not possible—a truth seeker sees his or her need for empowerment and those of a prospective truth teller as irreconcilably competitive—then the truth seeker probably expects very little. On the other hand, when a trusting relationship is desired or sought, then one's expectations for receiving the truth can run very high. In business settings this brings up a very interesting practical issue: Are people who desire trusting relationships necessarily on the hook to be honest and forthright in coming forward with the truth even when doing so places them and/or their projects in jeopardy? If your answer to this question is "No," then under what conditions is someone justified in withholding, bending, or misrepresenting the truth without severe costs to his or her organizational credibility or his or her relationship with truth seekers?

Thus, when it comes to building trusting relationships, the key truth-seeking issues become: "Given the concerns and special interests that underlie my professional pursuits and organizational commitments and the unique talents, strengths, and limitations I possess, and given the inevitability that the person from whom I am seeking the truth possesses at least somewhat different interests, commitments, talents, limitations, perceptions or situations and judgments, then (a) how much of the truth can I expect this person to tell me? and (b) under what conditions will this person feel sufficiently threatened to self-justify withholding, bending, or misrepresenting the truth?" In our minds these are pragmatic questions, not necessarily moral ones, which need answering before a manager can comprehend the quality of truth telling and the type of truth slipping that he or she should expect to receive.

The Stakes

On the truth teller's side, being open, honest, and forthcoming is easy to do when the personal costs for doing so are low, when the credibility costs of *not* telling the truth are high, or when telling the truth produces a relationship gain such as establishing oneself as credible and friendly in the truth seeker's eyes. However, when the costs of telling the truth are high—they place one's projects in jeopardy—then telling the truth becomes much more difficult to do. Once again keep in mind that we think truth telling entails substantially more than giving a direct response to a literal interpretation of the question asked. It entails volunteering information and perspective that is relevant to a truth seeker's needs even though that person has not thought to ask the specific question.

In work settings, what people see as the costs of telling the truth are too numerous for a finite listing. Some are obvious such as threat to a project, potential ammunition for the opposition, financial risks, personal security, increases in anxiety, losing one's competitive advantage, loss of control over the course events are taking, and even one's credibility with the other people on whom they are counting for support in portraying the "truth" a certain way. Many people have had the experience of hearing one associate tell another something like, "You weren't crazy enough to tell him *that*, were you?!" On the other hand, there are many nonobvious idiosyncratic costs to telling the truth which are impossible to comprehend before one knows a great deal about the specific people involved and what they have at stake in a particular situation.

What Is the Truth?

In theory there are at least four versions of the truth. First, there is "the truth as I think it." Second, there is "the truth as I decide you need to know it." Third, there is "the truth as you want to hear it told." And fourth, there is "the truth as I decide to tell it." To clarify, a brief illustration is provided.

> An example of the truth as I think it is: "There is no way that you are going to get promoted. No one thinks you have what it takes, myself included. Besides, you are a woman, and the first woman who makes assistant director is going to have to be a lot less controversial then you are."
>
> An example of the truth as I decide you need to know it is: "You asked 'how are you doing?' My answer is you are seen as very capable and developing."
>
> An example of the truth as you want to hear it is: "What you really want to hear is that while management sees you as making progress, and while we value the work we get from you, we see your chances of ever making the next management level as being somewhere between slim and none. But we don't want to tell you for fear of turning you off, and, in the process, possibly demotivating all the people working for you, and sending you on a job search before we are ready to do without you."
>
> An example of the truth as I decide to tell it to you, given my needs and what I know about you and your needs to know, is: "I *honestly*

can't tell you that you are assured of a promotion. This is a tough marketplace in which to predict company success. I'm going to say that you definitely possess upper management attributes, but the time is not quite right for me to strenuously push this. As far as your question about whether your situation warrants your buying a house and stretching yourself financially? If I were you I'd hold off because I see interest rates coming down and the mortgage lenders will be making much better deals."

In practice terms these four truth versions are so intermingled that people can never be sure of which truth version they are receiving or even the one they are giving. In fact, we believe that the politics inherent in one's organizational involvements make it very difficult for people to ever be 100 percent confident that they are providing the most honest version of the truth they know. On the other hand, people often report having another individual look them squarely in the eyes and speak sincerely implying that, to the best of his or her abilities, he or she is telling them the "truth" while they are convinced that the version of the truth they are receiving is not the "truth" as they need to hear it told.

Is it ever possible for a prospective truth seller to tell a truth seeker the *whole* truth and, if that can't be done, then how is a truth seeker ever going to hear the truth as he or she needs to hear it told? These questions are particularly relevant in the organizational realm where managers take pride in being action-oriented and efficient. Telling the whole truth is inefficient; it entails too much detail and requires too much time. Even if a prospective truth teller were so inclined, he or she could not be confident of supplying all the information that the truth seeker was pursuing. A truth teller can readily overlook stating something significant merely because that fact plays no significant role in the way he or she would ordinarily size up an organization event or orient to a job.

In organizations, most people are reconciled to seeking the "truth" as they think they need to hear it told. They do so by asking precise and focused questions aimed at forcing another individual to tell them what they want to know. Of course, by definition, this way of proceeding has built-in biases and limitations. One seldom learns more than what he or she is shrewd enough, in advance of the answer, to inquire about. And what is learned can get distorted by preconceived frameworks steeped in personal bias.

If asking precise and focused questions isn't a failsafe way to learn the truth, then is there a better way? A better way is for the potential truth teller to know enough about the truth seeker, his or her work orientation, professional objectives, and political realities to comprehend the deeper concerns that underlie that person's questions and, by virtue of being in a trusting relationship, to be motivated to address those issues. Only after a truth seeker has provided sufficient insight into his or her personal orientation and goals does a prospective truth teller have the potential to efficiently truth-tell. If the truth teller knows very little about the truth seeker, that person's orientation and the needs that underlie his or her questions, then it is unrealistic to expect the truth teller's answers to be more than statements of the truth as he or she decides the truth seeker needs to hear it told. And since the prospective truth teller's self-interests, personal resources, and organizational interests are all but guaranteed to be different from those of the truth seeker, then the "truth" the seeker receives is not necessarily going to be the version of the truth that person wants to hear.

This implies that it is the truth seeker's responsibility either to ask the precise questions that will retrieve what he or she wants to know or to provide a prospective truth teller with a sufficiently comprehensive background statement to allow the truth teller to comprehend the issues that underlie the questions being asked. And, as we've indicated, whether or not a truth seeker is inclined to reveal enough about his or her underlying motives to adequately cue a truth teller depends on the level of trust that already exists in the seeker's relationship with the teller. Thus truth telling and trust are interactive. Truth telling produces trust, and trust produces the capacity for truth telling.

The onus is on the truth seeker to open up first. However, we find that most people are involved in work relationships where trust is more a potential than a reality, and thus feel too vulnerable to divulge much background information. Consequently they take a course of extracting the truth through specific questions. Unfortunately, this way of proceeding can prove self-defeating since the skills that extract the truth often entail skepticism, cunning, and the asking of disarming and pointed questions that often inundate a relationship with distrust.

Thus, the possibility of a potential truth seller divulging the truth depends on the teller having sufficient understanding of the seeker's empowerment needs, as well as of the context within which that person seeks him- or herself operating. It also entails the teller knowing enough about the seeker's interests in the issue to accurately judge what is essential to relate. And, depending on the relationship, truth telling should even entail a volunteering of information. We have seen too many instances of people feeling betrayed and distrustful after discovering that some set of undisclosed facts were known by someone with whom they thought they had a "trusting relationship," and who they later thought only pretended not to understand the root of their inquiry, to limit truth telling to the criterion of merely providing an honest answer to the literal question asked.

Lies

At work is it ever acceptable for an individual to deliberately lie? Is it ever acceptable for an individual to calculatedly misrepresent? Is it ever acceptable for an individual to intentionally provide an altered version of the truth that was constructed to be beneficial for him or her at the expense of another person? In our experience there is a type of institutional double-think that strikes people who work in large organizations. People always expect the truth but they don't think they always have to give it. They expect the truth to the extent that they feel justified in punishing those who do not give it completely while, at the same time, admitting that no one in his or her right mind is going to truthfully tell me this or that and give me that much power at their own expense. People readily admit to thinking this way without perceiving any inconsistency.

Within any organization the ethic is absolute: It is *never* acceptable for someone to deliberately lie to you! And because people, especially managers, see themselves under an obligation to tell the truth, most are careful to maintain the cosmetics of truth telling even in moments when they consciously communicate "disinformation"— information that selected others will use to draw erroneous, self-defeating conclusions—in acts that are basically self-serving, territorial, and protectionistic. This is why, in organizations, people seldom get caught blatantly telling a lie. One merely observes them making *objective* interpretations that others see as excessively self-convenient, omitting nonessential elements of the story that are essential, or embroiled in *misunderstandings*, failing to recognize the underlying issue or question despite the fact that such a lack of recognition seems logically impossible. And the recipients of this type of treatment are careful not to say that someone lied. In organizations, everyone expects the other person to fight fire with fire; no one expects another person to automatically knuckle under to his or her power just because he or she was shrewd enough or quick enough to frame a truth-disclosing question.

Mistruths

"Mistruths" is the label we have given to the versions of the truth told by people who, in their own minds, are "truth tellers" but who find themselves in situations where their needs for empowerment, and their needs to avoid disempowerment, allow them to rationalize not telling the "entire" truth. They might reason, self-conveniently, that the other person didn't want or need to hear everything, that there is no good reason to make themselves vulnerable or to place their projects in jeopardy, or that their withholding the entire truth will cause the other person to act in an organizationally constructive way which they reason is in line with a higher set of values.

In theory it is very difficult for us to distinguish between the negative impact of a lie and a mistruth. We consider a conscious and deliberate misrepresentation of the facts to accomplish a self-convenient end to be a "lie." We consider versions of the truth that may be literally true but are manipulative in that they aren't sufficient to allow the truth seeker to conclude as he or she would have concluded with the prospective truth-teller's access to the facts to be "mistruths." Nevertheless, we find that in practical day-to-day organizational dealings every manager makes a distinction. Managers with the highest values and strongest personal commitments to integrity are able to rationalize mistruths on the grounds of establishing or preserving their personal and organizational empowerment.

We have already mentioned many of the ways that people communicate mistruths. The three most popular ones are intentionally self-convenient portrayals of the "truth," calculatedly timed disclosure of selected elements of the truth, and the intentional feigning of agreement when the discloser's private sentiments are in opposition. Elsewhere (Culbert & McDonough, 1980) we have termed these three forms of mistruths "framing," "fragmenting," and "playing-it-both ways." Each are commonly used mechanisms which everyone who works in an organization, especially middle- and upper-level managers, count on for their daily survival and engage in with little apprehension that they are telling a lie. In organizations, people mislead one another all the time. They do so with few pangs of conscience believing that the success of their unit's projects and their personal image and survival depend on their ability to manipulate others and to manage their relationships with them.

Role-Generated Mistruths

In most organizations there are numerous daily instances of people believing that they are in a situation that requires them not to tell the truth as they know it, or as they know the seeker desires to hear it, that gets justified on the "higher" grounds of performing one's job well. These are role-generated mistruths. Examples include: the salesman who embellishes the merits of a $129.00 item without divulging that this item will be reduced to $64.50 when the store-wide half-price sale beings in two days; the boss who plans to dismiss an employee in three months and who, in order to avoid the person leaving early, converses with that employee as if his or her job will last forever; and the politician who earnestly advocates a position that he or she does not inwardly embrace believing that such a public endorsement is required to achieve the voter support he or she needs. Within organizations, people are ever seeking to "manage the news" and to "reconstruct history" in an effort to create the images and impressions that will allow them to perform competently and experience personal and project success. And they often do this feeling fully justified because, in their minds, they are merely following the institutional prescription for doing their job well and getting ahead.

Unconscious Mistruths

Only occasionally can prospective truth tellers relate more of the truth than they themselves consciously realize. They do this by providing facts that allow a truth seeker to piece together an enlightened interpretation for him- or herself. Thus, when truth seekers engage an individual whom they feel has failed to think through an issue sufficiently to provide them a valid perspective, or someone whom they believe has misconcluded, or someone who, for reasons of personality, they see as unable to face up to the reality of the facts, truth seekers feel they have no alternative but to search for the truth themselves. Often they can accomplish this by asking numerous questions that meticulously piece together elements of the answer they are searching out. However, as we mentioned, proceeding this way communicates a lack of trust which strains their relationship with their would-be informant. The point here is that it is much easier to form trusting and truth-telling relationships with people who are self-reflective, conscious, and informed.

On the other hand, truth seekers may misperceive a situation by thinking that they are encountering an unconscious mistruth when in fact the other person has sufficient awareness of the "truth" and, for one reason or another, has decided to selectively withhold it while giving the impression that he or she is telling everything. In such situations, the truth seeker's questioning and the reluctant informant's desire to withhold produce an intellectual chess match of wits.

The Truth Seeker's Obligation

To this point some readers may have gotten the impression that we think that truth telling is primarily the responsibility either of the truth teller or the truth seeker. This is not how we see it. We believe that the *relationship* between the truth teller and the truth seeker produces both the version of the truth that is told and the version of the truth that is heard.

We believe that there are internal and external limitations on the brand of truth a potential truth teller can tell and that a truth seeker should consider these limitations and compensate for them when listening for the "truth." Learning what those needs and limitations are is the responsibility of the truth seeker.

We also believe that a truth teller who seriously desires to tell the truth has a responsibility to learn enough about the needs and orientation of the truth seeker, otherwise the brand of truth he or she tells is likely to be rooted more in his or her needs and orientation than in those of the truth seeker.

Thus we believe that, in an organization, there is a great deal that the truth seeker needs to comprehend and superimpose on the information he or she receives to compensate for the truth teller's personal limitations, professional biases, organizational commitments, and what that person sees as the political realities with which he or she must deal in order to function effectively. Conversely, we believe that there is a great deal that a potential truth teller needs to learn about the personal, professional, and organizational commitments of the so-called truth seeker before he or she can know which facts are essential to that person. And we believe that both individuals' abilities to understand the background and situational factors underlying the other person's needs for empowerment will directly determine the extent to which the two are able to form a trusting relationship.

THE DECISION TO TELL THE TRUTH

In discussing the dynamics of truth telling we hope we have not misled some readers into thinking that we sanction not telling the truth. To the contrary, our viewpoint has always been that long-term personal and organizational effectiveness requires truth telling and that high-quality truth telling depends on people forming trusting relationships. However, we find that "practical necessities" and "experiences" of organization life can cause otherwise high-integrity people to *slip* telling one another the truth, to get taken in by the words that are spoken and to *slip* hearing the truth, and, on both parts, to self-justify their truth-slipping actions. We see people who don't speak the truth self-justifying their actions on the grounds of functioning effectively and doing what the institution needs; and we see people who aren't able to elicit the truth failing to recognize the practical and personal effectiveness issues faced by the other person and justifying their subsequent indignation and their retaliatory distortion of the truth on grounds that the other person deliberately misled them.

Our major point has been that truth telling and truth interpreting do not reach their potential because so many people who set out to tell and hear the truth get confused by what is actually entailed in achieving a truthful exchange. People get confused by moral imperatives to tell the truth which misled them to think that they are telling the truth, or receiving it, even when the truth is being slipped. People get confused by the immediate practical issues entailed in being a success and functioning with empowerment that allows them to put a relativity factor into their telling the truth. And people get confused by the fact that telling the truth and one's life involvements and inner motives are so intertwined that the "brand" of truth one is telling, or is being told, is determined by too many factors to have them all conscious simultaneously. People are impacted by organizational responsibilities, expectations to perform, personal needs, political considerations, and, most importantly, by their relationships with the people who are questioning them.

We find that most people suspect as much, based on what they think when they are a potential truth teller on the receiving end of a truth seeker's questions. When asked a question, they think "Who wants to know and why is this person asking me?" They think "How will the answer I'm inclined to give affect me personally?" and, we would add, "politically?" And they think "How will the answer I am inclined to give affect my relationship with that person as well as with others who are also important to me?"

The question "Who wants to know and why is this person asking?" bears on what the potential truth teller sees as the legitimacy of the inquiry being directed his or her way. The potential truth teller scrutinizes the organizational reasons for giving a complete answer and addresses not just the question but the spirit behind the question which is usually centered on the empowerment motives of the truth seeker. Despite countless and well-publicized examples to the contrary, we find that most people take their organizational citizenship very seriously. They would prefer to provide others with the information they request. And usually, they do so when provided the organizational effectiveness reasons embedded in the truth seeker's request. Of course when it comes to telling the truth, one's organizational responsibilities become a double-edged sword. People can just as readily cite organizational responsibilities that justify why they gave versions of the truth that misled.

The question "How does the answer I am inclined to give affect me personally (and politically)?" relates to an individual's need to function competently and successfully both in terms of personal meaning and organizational success. One's perceptions of what the truth is and his or her decisions of how to portray and communicate what he or she sees as the truth are always colored by how that individual views his or her empowerment needs being served.

In organizations people may readily agree on objectives. But the resources people have, and the means they use in addressing agreed-upon objectives are as different as their thumb prints. People with different ways of being competent and different needs for empowerment see organizational situations differently and vie to get organizational events framed in ways that provide them the context they require for personal success. This, incidentally, is the basis of organizational politics, a topic we continue to research (Culbert & McDonough, 1985, 1986, 1988). Organizational politics are the conversations, manipulations, and actions that take place as people with different self-interests, who consequently see the same organizational events differently, attempt to frame those events consistently with their needs for personal success and organizational acceptance.

The question "How will the answer I am inclined to give affect my relationship with this person as well as with others who also are important to me?" is interpersonally directed and, at its core, a political one. While every organizational transaction has an immediate outcome dimension, other, often more critical, dimensions are also at stake. At stake are an individual's organizational image and credibility with onlookers, not just his or her relationship with the person asking the questions. In fact, sometimes the agendas of others who are invisible to the immediate situation are the most important influences to recognize in understanding the brand of truth the would-be truth teller decides to provide. It's rare for managers to suspend thinking about their image and credibility and the roles others play in their success. They think about how others see them, what others are inclined to do for them, and how they have to be seen in order to insure that these others give them what they need. They give these others serious consideration before transacting on even the seemingly simplest and most straightforward of organizational communications, and even with people whose association with these others is remote.

CONCLUSION

If, in an organization, there was an absolute obligation to tell the truth, where each individual felt compelled to truthfully answer each question asked him or her, then people would experience themselves as powerless. They could never count on controlling a situation long enough to operate with empowerment. On the other hand, if people were without the standard expectation that every question they asked would receive a truthful response, then people would also experience themselves as powerless. They could not rationally reason through a situation because at any point a critical "fact," on which they were preceding, might turn out to be false.

In today's organizations, we find that most people manipulate in seeking and telling the truth. They feel they must do so in order to operate with sufficient power to be effective. They put energy into phrasing questions that they hope will force the truth from people who are not inclined to give it to them. They put energy into phrasing answers that shade what they know as the truth in directions that prove personally and organizationally empowering to them.

On the other hand, most people also work hard to build relationships and to develop the conditions that allow them, progressively, to operate with more and more candor. They find out more about the other person's needs for their "truthful" inputs, and they find out more about the built-in biases and ways of perceiving the world that the other person superimposes on what he or she thinks is the truth.

Thus, we see truth telling as a process in which *both* the truth teller and the truth seeker have responsibilities. We see the needs of both frustrated as long as situations are structured so that one person's seeking of the truth and the other's telling of it come at a disadvantage to the empowerment needs of either. In contrast, relationships in which both participants are looking to empower the other build an atmosphere of trust that make synergistic statements of the turth—ones that simultaneously relate to the needs of the truth seeker and the perceptions of the truth teller—more possible.

REFERENCES

Bennett, A. (1988, April 22). When the boss is bedridden. *The Wall Street Journal*, pp. 15R–18R.
Bok, S. (1982). *Secrets*. New York: Pantheon Books.

Bok, S. (1978). *Lying: Moral choice in public and private life*. New York: Pantheon Books.

Culbert, S. A., & McDonough, J. J. (1988) Organizational alignments, schisms, and high integrity managerial behavior. In S. Srivastra (Ed.), *The functioning of executive integrity*. San Francisco: Jossey-Bass.

Culbert, S. A., & McDonough, J. J. (1986) The politics of trust and organization empowerment. *Public Administration Quarterly, 2,* 171–189.

Culbert, S. A., & McDonough, J. J. (1985). *Radical management: Power, politics, and the pursuit of trust*. New York: The Free Press.

Culbert, S. A., & McDonough, J. J. (1980). *The invisible war: Pursuing self-interests at work*. New York: John Wiley.

Gibb, J. R. (1978). *Trust: A new view of personal and organizational development*. Los Angeles: Guild of Tutors Press.

Goffman, E. (1959). *The presentation of self in everyday life*. Garden City, NY: Doubleday Anchor.

Shultz, G. (1987, June). Testimony presented to The Select Committee Of The House And Senate Investigating The Iran-Contra Affair.

Speakes, L. (1988). *Speaking out*. New York: Charles Scribner's Sons.

9

The Other Impossible Profession

Joseph Luft
Berkeley, CA

OD consultation is a young profession confronted by great opportunities and racked by many dilemmas. Some of the dilemmas are shared with other fields in the helping professions; others are unique to this field. I feel quite certain that each OD practitioner has his own list of predicaments, and I shall attempt to identify a few of my favorites. I begin with some observations by Freud on the profession he himself invented.

OD consultation was not what Freud had in mind when he said,

> Here let us pause for a moment to assure the analyst that he has our sincere sympathy in the very exacting demands he has to fulfill in carrying out his activities. It almost looks as if analysis were the third of those "impossible" professions in which one can be sure beforehand of achieving unsatisfying results. The other two, which have been known much longer, are education and government. (Freud, 1933/1964, p. 248)

But what would Freud call a profession that combines all three? Clearly, OD consultation is concerned with learning (education), with organization and bureaucracy (government), and of course with individual awareness and insight, growth and change (psychotherapy).

Who is the OD consultant and what are his or her qualifications to meet the requirements of this impossible profession?

Freud answers (paraphrasing), "Obviously we cannot demand that the prospective '*OD consultant*' (oops! make that 'analyst') should be a perfect being before he takes up analysis, in other words that only persons of such high and rare perfection should enter the profession." O.K. So the prospective OD consultant is not perfect. What about training for the profession? Freud states the matter simply, "But where and how is the poor wretch to acquire the ideal qualifications which he will need in his profession?"

We are not surprised at Freud's answer: "The answer is, in an analysis of himself, with which his preparation for this future activity begins. For practical reasons this analysis can only be short and incomplete" (Freud, 1933/1964, p. 249). And a bit later, Freud recommends that "every analyst should periodically—at intervals of five years or so—submit himself to analysis once more without feeling ashamed of taking this step" (p. 249). Training has accomplished its purpose, Freud continues, when the analyst begins "to perceive in himself things which would otherwise be incredible to him." By now, everyone is familiar with the inevitable distortions, biases, denials and projections with which each of us, consultants and clients alike, protect ourselves. And one of the main occupational hazards in the impossible professions, Freud warns, is "that when a man is endowed with power it is hard for him not to misuse it" (1933/1964, p. 249).

Handing over the mantle of expert authority on organizations and their work to the OD consultant, along with the latter's temptation to use it, is an occupational hazard painfully familiar to people in the OD field. But what's a client to do? Stressed by organizational and interpersonal problems of all kinds, the client turns for help to some expert with a degree or two in Organizational Development, whatever that is. The client knows from experience that he can get help from a lawyer, a doctor, a dentist, an engineer, by turning over the problem and letting the experts handle it. But an OD consultant?

Explaining, teaching and counseling the client(s) on what OD is about while at the same time assessing the situation is not easy. Naturally, how we as consultants do what we do is crucial. The attitudes, feelings, and values expressed, particularly in the initial meetings with clients, are fundamental to the entire consultation. We are building a working relationship; we are becoming informed about the client and the initial picture of the problem; and we are conveying to the client that she/he has come to the right person for help.

OD—NO ROAD MAPS

Trying to make sense of the problems from the clients' point of view while figuring out what's really going on in the organization is like trespassing in a fertile swamp while trying to fly a kite. Road maps may not help too much either, but ideas and theories and models do serve as indispensable guidelines in strange territory. Even though the theories and models are limited and peppered with sundry mythologies, and even when they do not fit quite right, they enable the consultant to probe—to find out who and what might be relevant—and to generate more information and attitudes about life in the organization.

Suggestions by the consultant to bring together certain members of the organization in order to gather and exchange information, clarify issues, and open up denied or ignored differences constitute a core aspect of OD work. Here again the consultant must be in two places at once, that is, listening to and emphasizing with clients, while thinking about the next appropriate steps. As Mary Weisbord (1987, p. 15) describes it, "The best role the consultant can hope for is stage manager." Watching clients respond to the freeing effect of task-oriented work can be one of the most gratifying experiences of the OD consultant's job. But it is also obviously not entirely controllable or predictable—and may not always function successfully. Despite some new learnings, even insights, changes, and bursts of euphoria along the way, experienced consultants know that meaningful organizational change and development can take a long time—even years.

RAPID CHANGE

The acceleration of change in business and technology creates additional dilemmas for the consultant. While serious organizational development may take a long time, business and commerce are hard-pressed for rapid changes and quick results. Recent stock market crashes involving the yen, the mark, and the dollar, interacting instantly and simultaneously, have brought this home all too vividly. The stock market is both symbolic and symptomatic of the speed of change in business and industry: changes in ownership and power, mergers and transfers, shifts in hierarchical positioning, as well as new technologies and changes in consumer trends.

Though speed of change does not have a destabilizing effect on organizations and on the work of the OD consultant, the real problem as seen by managers and executives is economic survival. And when the black ink turns red, industries and businesses tend to tighten reins. Cutbacks in jobs, transfers, reassignments, and pay reductions may dominate the action. Ironically, in that climate, just when intrinsic motivation needs to be strengthened through mutual support and collaboration to help bring out the most effective productivity, the opposite occurs. Management tends to shift toward Theory X. Employees are threatened and often feel as if they were under siege. As reported in the *Washington Post*, for example, many organizations cut back on employees with "chain saw sensitivity." And as one professor of business put it, "It's a more hard spirited attitude than I've ever seen in a long time."

OD CONSULTATION IN THE SERVICE
OF BUREAUCRACY

OD staff, especially in-house professionals, if they are not fired as part of the cutbacks, are sometimes pressed into bureaucratic control activities, using techniques such as job analysis, performance evaluation, tests and measurements. Here we run into another dilemma. For some professionals, tests and measures are just a regular part of the OD job. However, for an increasing number of consultants and other applied psychologists, personality measures, and aptitude and achievement tests are of double scientific value. But what is even worse, there is a growing realization that these instruments are used in the service of power and politics (within the organization to induce willing cooperation and docility of employees (See Holloway, 1984).

VALUES AND ROLES

Values in practice constitute another major source of problems for the OD consultant. I want to avoid straying beyond the scope of this chapter except to say that the consultant's role is loaded with questions of values and ethics. It is understandable that since management hires or contracts with the OD consultant, the productivity-related interests of management would strongly influence the OD work, more so than considerations of mental health, the work environment, family relations of employees, or trade unions. Though these sets of interests may carry different weight for leaders in the organization and for employees at any given time, they are not necessarily incompatible. Still, the OD consultant may agonize over the fact that she/he is at times powerless to do anything about them.

Robert Bellah, U.S. sociologist, in his recent *Habits of the Heart* (1985) addressed a closely related issue. He and his colleagues point out that psychologists do tend to get caught up in the effort to produce "the coolly manipulative style of management." To the extent that objectivity and utilitarian values, so important to the engineer, scientist, and technician, spread to human relations at home as well as at work, serious malaise will increase. The manager and the OD consultant in collusion, mostly unintended, may actually foster and legitimize the "autonomous individual and the cooly manipulative style." We join with Bellah in deploring the practices involved even as we strive to better understand and to appreciate the reality of this dilemma.

FAMILY BUSINESSES

As if to further confound the problem of job roles and values carrying over to home and community, we have to take account of the fact that it's a two-way street. Family businesses, for example, may be affected by relationships and emotional problems at home more so than by the technical organizational issues, according to a *Wall Street Journal* report. If, as *Family Business Review* claims, ninety percent of all businesses are family owned, employ about half the work force—including one third of the Fortune 500 corporations—and account for half the gross national product, then clearly family-run businesses are not a trivial matter, and must be understood by I/O psychology in general and by OD consultants in particular. When family-run businesses need help, the OD consultant may be one of the few professionals who can offer useful assistance. Emotional ties and conflicts within the family cannot be ignored, and generational transitions and their effects on organizational policy and control need to be understood. For the stout-hearted OD specialist, consulting with family-run businesses offers a resounding set of challenges, both to serve and to learn. Other OD consultants, perhaps not quite so bold or experienced, should not be chastized for ruminating or even chanting, "Oh Lord . . . family hierarchies, sibling rivalry, Oh Oedipus in the board room, where is Dr. Freud when we need him now?"

OD AND THE TIES THAT BIND

OD consultation is directly affected by the willingness of employees to cooperate with one another. After all, organizations exist in order to produce goods and services through collaborative arrangements with people and technology. Fifty years after the Hawthorne Electric studies, it seems banal to talk abut the importance of people's feelings and sense of connectedness to one another on the job or in the community. And yet many informed observers, in addition to social scientists such as Robert Bellah, believe that we may be undergoing significant changes in our culture, changes which are affecting organizations in a profound way. Scandals in Wall Street and in high government office are the most obvious examples of violations of trust and fair play. What is perhaps still more serious as far as the immediate future is concerned deals with college students.

According to a survey of nearly 290,000 students nationwide conducted by the American Council on Education in 1987, only 40% chose "developing a meaningful philosophy of life" as a personal goal compared to over 80% just twenty years ago. Also the number of students choosing future careers in business more than doubled over what it was two decades ago. What this means is summarized by the director of the study, Professor Alexander Astin (1988, p. 2): "The trend is a profound shift not only in students' values but also in the values of the larger society." Astin agrees with Bellah that as a society we have moved sharply away from concern with each other and with community, and toward more self-concern and interest in money matters. These attitudes may again be shifting.

TOWARD A MAIN OD FOCUS

Thee changes in social values taken together with greater transiency in job and organizational lifespan are being felt in OD work such as team building and various other collaborative efforts. In addition, with new professions emerging in the service and information technology industries, many employees have shifted loyalty from a particular firm to their professional associations, very much as academics tend to do. A work relationship in a sound organization was always considered a compact of some mutual understanding based on fair play and trust and a sense of interpersonal loyalty. Without these ties, the bonds that hold an organization and indeed, a nation, together and enable it to function, become problematic. The atmosphere changes and cynicism spreads.

If I were to identify one central focus for the OD consultant, I would say it is concern for trust. To be sure, the technical and social systems in their uniqueness to specific organizational problems must be understood and addressed. But without that assurance, that is, some confidence in the consultant's relationship with clients, there is not much holding the fabric of OD work together.

How can the OD consultant manage to counteract the spread of cynicism? Can I/O psychology offer the necessary science, and OD the necessary skill to do the job? No. That would not be enough. What makes the effort feasible is a hidden hunger waiting to be nourished. Hidden hunger? Yes. Within each person and within each group and within each organization is a hunger for some faith and confidence and trust in others. Find a way to nourish that hunger and the consultation will have a chance to thrive. Each consultant must find his/her own way to earn the trust of clients. That's what makes it difficult. That's what makes it satisfying. That's why it's called the other impossible profession.

REFERENCES

Astin, A. (1988, January 14). American Council on Education. San Francisco Chronicle, p. 2.

Bellah, R. N. (1985). *Habits of the heart.* Madsen, R., Sullivan, W. M., Swidler, A., & Tipton, S. M. Berkeley: University of California Press.

Freud, S. (1964). Analysis terminable and interminable. In J. Strachey (Ed. and Trans.), The standard edition of the complete psychological works of Sigmund Freud (Vol. 22). London: Hogarth Press. (Original publication 1933)

Holloway, W. (1984). Fitting work: Psychological assessment in organizations. In J. Henriques (Ed.), *Changing the subject.* London: Methuen.

Weisbord, M. R. (1987, Winter). Toward third wave managing and consulting. *Organizational Dynamics*, p. 15.

10

How to Use Laboratory Learning

Sherman Kingsbury
Mill Valley, CA

HOW TO USE MEMORIES FROM EXPERIENCES IN GROUPS

Experience is the most important single source of learning I have. From one point of view, the simple accumulation of conscious and unconscious memories of events constitutes my learning from those experiences. But probably a more important part is my remembered reaction to the events. The remembered reactions are more important because I often repeat those same reactions in a new situation, even if the first experience is not in my conscious awareness. Something in the new experience evokes the old reaction, even if the connection is not made consciously.

Learning from experiences takes place when the reaction to an event is conditioned both by what I have learned in the past and by the unique and special qualities of the event itself. My memories of events as well as my reactions to events are both selective and interpretative. They are selective in the sense that only certain aspects of events are remembered while others are quite forgotten. They are interpretative in that different individuals will have different feelings and make different judgments about what appears to be the same experience. These feelings, judgments, and attitudes may emerge later in similar situations and influence the reactions I have to them. It is easy to see how learning from experience can become blocked and can lapse into learning the same thing over and over, not so much because the same experiences keep happening again and again as because the same reactions keep happening again and again, and the freshness and uniqueness of the new experience is not taken into account in shaping the new reaction.

When one is able to bring his or her reaction to an experience into full conscious awareness, relating the current reaction to the original experiences that gave rise to it, then it is possible to grasp the freshness and learning opportunity in the new experience and to allow new reactions that are appropriate to the new experience.

It is interesting to speculate about what aspects of two situations make them so similar to the individual that the reactions from the prior situation are evoked in the latter one. One person may link situations because the emotional climate of the two seems alike. Another may link them because their logic is the same. Still another may link them because they seem to have the same kind of power relationships. The particular way a person links situations in his or her associative memory may provide clues to to deep elements of his personality and character. That is what makes personal learning from experience very much an individual matter.

NONVERBAL MEMORIES

Often in my daily life, particularly at moments when I am struggling to understand what is going on in a situation, an image or a scene from the past keeps appearing in my mind. It is almost as if a mental video recording of the past event intrudes into my awareness. When that happens, I can choose to ignore it, treating it as some random or unwanted signal, or I can regard it as a message from myself, alerting me to the possibility that there is something in the image that has significance for the present situation. When I am able to pay attention to this memory and try to understand what it is that some part of me sees as related about the two situations, I can often find a greater clarity about how to deal with the present situation.

EXAMPLES

A T-group is a situation which involves ambiguity, strong feelings, intense interpersonal interactions, and much that is new and unfamiliar. It is rich in new and challenging events, and it occurs in a setting that encourages one to become aware of his full reaction to what is going on. Thus a T-group experience is a rich environment in which to produce memories that may be evoked associatively in the future.

There are some scenes from training laboratories that enter my mind fairly often and when they do, they instruct me:

I often see in my mind's eye a lady I met once. She is standing, looking at a group and speaking. As she speaks, she gestures, starting with her hands close in front of her chest with her palms facing the group. Her arms move forward and then out toward the side, still with her palms facing the group. It is as though she is pushing something away from her. While she makes this gesture, she says, "I just love to get close to people." As I think about the event, I remember that I had felt uneasy with her before that. But with those two messages, one from her hands and its opposite from her words, I understood my uneasiness. Now, when she comes to mind, I start looking for unconsciously communicated double messages, either those that I am sending, or those of others.

Sometimes, it is just the words that someone has said that provide the help, often just a bit of theory or a concept. But even then, when the words come to mind, they usually appear in a scene with a real, remembered speaker. One such vision is that of a rather exasperated person saying, "Well, it isn't the tools that build the house . . . " He comes into my mind's eye often. When he does, he usually catches me in a situation where I or someone else is losing sight of the purpose, the vision, or the energy in a situation because of a preoccupation with techniques.

I have often been in situations where I am impatient to realize the full results of what has been done. At such times, Douglas McGregor may appear in my inner vision. We were talking at the end of my first T-group. I was saying that I doubted that I was yet feeling the full impact of the experience. He said, "I hope it takes years for the dust to settle." He was right. It has taken years. More importantly, his statement often comes up to warn me against being too impatiently anxious to conclude in other situations.

It is easy for me to become defensive or retaliatory when I think I am being attacked or rejected. In some such situations, I remember a time when I was substituting briefly for the regular leader of a group. A man said to me, "I do not think I trust you. You are sitting in Bill's chair." Before I could get fully mobilized for defense, someone in the group asked me how that made me feel. Instead of behaving automatically the way I often do when I feel attacked or rejected, I began paying attention to how I was feeling. And while the defensiveness was there, I also found a certain liking for the man who said he did not trust me. I felt I could trust him to let me know where I stood with him. I felt a little safer in that strange situation because of him.

The need for approval is so great in me that I have to keep relearning the value of honest information about where I stand with people, and the memory of that man has helped me often. But there have also been times when that message from myself simply served to remind me to pay attention to all my feelings and not unthinkingly lock into my defensive reactions.

USING THEORIES, CONCEPTS AND TECHNIQUES

Another part of my learning from laboratory experiences has come in the form of theories, principles, concepts and techniques. I have a lot of trouble making practical use of these, because in the real-world situation when I most need help, my anxiety or my great need to keep my precious ego from being bruised tends to make it hard to devote attention to thinking about concepts, theories, or techniques.

Yet concepts and theories are powerful tools that can help me transform myself and my relationships. For a concept to be useful to me, it needs to be brief, compressed into a few words, or better yet into a vivid image or word picture. I need to be able to hold all of it in mind at once and not have to work to rehearse the steps when I need them. When I can hold it in mind all at once and not have the memory distract too much attention from the ongoing events, then the concept becomes a gentle prod to my intellect and a guide to action.

Take the concept of trust, for example. Trust is very important. People often talk about the need to increase it or to build it. It is often a critical factor in successful human affairs. There is a conceptual statement about trust that I am able to remember at critical times in the middle of things:

> Trust increases when trusting actions meet with trust-worthy responses.

I can even allow a little elaboration of this idea and still keep it in mind when I need it:

> Trusting actions call for risk-taking and that requires courage. Trustworthy responses call for commitment and that involves self-discipline.

But even when I can only hang onto the first part, that brief statement about trust tells me that if I want to experience more trust in a situation, there are some specific things I can do about it.

Here is another concept that I can only rarely capture when I most need it:

> Ordinarily, another person's defenses are not defending against me, they are defending that person against his own anxiety.

When I can remember that, I gain some control over my own defensiveness, because I can remember to look into what in the situation seems to be making me anxious, rather than struggling to protect myself against what the other person seems to be doing to me.

Here is another: At one time or another, most of us find ourselves trying to figure out what another person's motives are. There is a test of such an ascription that keeps me from making a lot of mistakes about other people's motives, if only I can keep it in mind:

> Be sure that the motives you ascribe to another are ones that person could think of himself as having.

The use of learned techniques raises a problem if it cannot be done in a way that is fresh and spontaneous. Not that freshness and spontaneity should be valued for themselves alone, but things feel better when they are fresh and spontaneous. To plan ahead of time that you will probably use a particular technique in a group situation makes sense, provided you can be open and alert in the actual situation and only use the technique if it feels right in real time.

Richard Farson has said that in important human affairs striving to learn techniques is a dead-end approach. The struggle is to learn to be fully in the present for the event, with all faculties available and open to the essential uncertainties in the situation. This approach provides the freshness and spontaneity that brings the needed creativity and intuition to important human events. Farson's aphorism, "Technique converts romance into seduction," brilliantly captures this point in easy-to-remember form.

But what do you do with the techniques that you know? I often find myself in situations where particular techniques or approaches keep intruding themselves into my thinking. When that happens, I try to look closely at what is going on to see why I am reminded of my technique and why it might apply in this situation. Then I ask myself if it needs to be modified or adapted to fit the unique needs of this situation. And then I wait, and sometimes events will take a turn so that it feels right and fresh and spontaneous to use the technique.

There are several theories of group development. Some of them parse out a group's life into many stages and substages. If one can get enough distance from groups, or can live with such a theory long enough that it is well internalized, it can be very helpful. But a short, deceptively simple theory of group development can also be very helpful:

Groups (meetings and relationships, too) have a beginning, a middle, and an end.

Just thinking about that reminds me to ask myself which of those phases I am in and to wonder whether I am trying to do the middle part without having experienced the beginning.

Most organizational theory is so complex that I can not begin to achieve active mastery over it. Yet there are some helpful perspectives provided by short simple statements:

> In decision-making, when how the decision is implemented is critical to its outcome, the commitment of the group to the decision is generally more important to the outcome than is the detailed quality of the decision.

Or,

> As organizations become more competent, they don't stop having problems; instead, they recognize and try to cope with better problems.

These examples are a few of the conceptual or theoretical nuggets from my experience that I find are "mind-graspable" enough so that I can make real use of them. Making a conscious effort to glean, refine, and polish these nuggets is a way to gain a better chance to make effective behavioral use of theory and ideas derived from both formal and informal learning situations.

Using concepts in this way is quite different from using pieces of conceptual jargon to call other people names. I am thinking of statements such as: "You are a 1,1 while I am a 9,9." Or, "Why are you so defensive?" Or, "You are at the oral stage." It is easy to detect this kind of use of concepts because the speaker always seems to see himself on a slightly higher level than the person addressed.

Trying to be systematic about panning one's experience for 'conceptual nuggets' is, I believe, a useful approach to self-development.

THE USE OF INSIGHT

Insight is another major feature of experiential learning. I experience two quite different kinds of insight. The first is a begrudging, painful kind of admission about myself that leaves me feeling shame or guilt or remorse about the way I have been. In the second kind, I greet discovery with a sense of delight and wonder. Laughter and pleasure of discovery are inherent in this kind of insight. It is just this pleasure in discovery that may explain why the "ha-ha" of laughter and the "aha!" of discovery appear to be so close together in the language.

The painful kind of insight is hard to make use of. It creates New Year's resolutions and control systems, and a feeling of being forced to use the insight. It often has the quality of being painted onto you from the outside by other people who are trying to force you to believe it. In the end, making use of this kind of insight often takes more energy that it is worth.

But the Aha! of discovery leading to the Ha-Ha! of delight seems to have some quite different, wonderful and mysterious qualities. First of all, you don't have to *do* anything to make use of this kind of insight. You don't have to struggle to apply it. It has a marvelous way of making itself effective. The task with this kind of insight is not to capture or to take advantage of it; the task is just to experience it.

The thing that appears to make the difference between the two types of insight is one's attitude toward the self. Do I see myself as a flawed thing, a fake disguised as human, afraid of being unmasked before you or before myself? If instead I can see myself as a full member of the human race, then whatever I do or feel is a natural part of the human condition. I can examine whatever I have done with friendly interest and a spirit of inquiry, rather than with harsh judgment and a sense of alienation from myself. With this attitude, my direction for movement is to become as genuinely, directly, unabashedly human as I can possibly be.

SELF AS INSTRUMENT

Gurjieff enjoined his students to "Remember yourself." Your experience is already a part of yourself, and the events, feelings, and concepts are already recorded in your being. The problem is remembering yourself, getting your ego and its ideas about how you would like to appear out of the way, and allowing what has become you to emerge and flower. It is no work to remember to use your experience. If you stay out of its way, you already *are* your experience. If you are objective enough, acceptant enough, and internally quiet enough, then you can remember yourself, and your recorded experiences are already part of you, available for use.

The self is the instrument of action in human affairs. It is the self who leads and follows, who teaches and learns, who loves and hates, who helps and is helped. There is much talk about the development of skills and techniques. But the real object of development is the self.

In thinking about the self, I get the image of an ancient castle, spread over several hills, with endless number of rooms and winding corridors. In a few of those rooms a light is shining, a light which allows one to explore and study those rooms, those aspects of the self. I think of development of the self as bringing the light into more rooms to allow discovery of what is already there but as yet unrealized.

Mostly the discovery and recognition of the self occurs through relationships with other people. Relationships provide the foundation for the self to distinguish between reality and fantasy and to receive nourishment for growth.

OBJECTIVE OBSERVATION OF THE SELF

In the quest for learning, for getting the most out of experience, the first task is to make the experience conscious and to be able to separate what is happening from one's own reactions to what is happening. Equally important is using my observations of myself and the observations others make of me to discover how my responses are distorting my perceptions and my attitudes toward my experience. Becoming objective in this way requires that I separate myself from my grasping ego's need to look good or to feel perfect and to come to accept myself for what I really am, for what I am becoming. To the extent I can do this, the meaning of my experience is then available to me.

Still, in using my experience, that is to say, in learning from my experience, I need to permit myself to remember events as they were, to give up censoring myself from past behavior, and simply to pay objective attention to what I remember and search for its relationship to my current situation. I need to allow myself to enjoy the discoveries I make about myself, even if they are hard on my precious ego. I need to accept myself as a developing human being, always with much still to discover.

I need to make use of my cognitive mind to form conceptual encapsulations of my experience, refining these encapsulations far enough that I can hold them before me in my awareness at the times of action when I need them.

Laboratory learning is directed at the self. Its basic goal is a metagoal, that of learning how to learn about the self. Its basic method is to create a context in which the focus is on learning about the self, while simultaneously paying attention to how self-learning takes place. This allows the process of self-learning to be transferred to others, everyday contexts.

The tools of self-learning are:

- An objective, inquisitive interest in being aware of your own behavior and what underlies it.
- An active and objective interest in how others see and interpret your behavior, to help you gain more facility in having other people react to you in the way you intend.
- Openness to ideas and images that come to mind so that they can be used as a guide in current situations.
- An internalized grasp of powerful concepts and theories as that are poignant enough and brief enough to be able to influence your behavior in action situations.

Author Index

Subject Index